D0129305

DELICIOUS DONE EASY

100+ Surprising & Simple
One-Pot Recipes

Copyright © 2017 SharkNinja Operating LLC

All rights reserved. No portion of this book may be reproduced by any means whatsoever without written permission from SharkNinja Operating LLC, except for the inclusion of quotations in a media review.

Editors and Content: Meghan Reilly, Kenzie Swanhart, and Elizabeth Skladany

Recipe Development: Amy Golino, Sam Ferguson, Molly Shuster, Joy Howard, Judy Cannon, Irina Margil and Great Flavors

Design and Layout: Emily Regis and Lisa Vroman

Copywriter: Melissa Stefanini

Creative Director: Joshua Hanson

Photo Direction: Joshua Hanson and Dmitry Mangeym

Photography: Molly Shuster, Joy Howard, and Shutterstock

Published in the United States of America by
SharkNinja Operating LLC
89 A Street
Needham, MA 02494

CS960 ISBN: 978-1-5323-4244-8

NINJA is a registered trademark of SharkNinja Operating LLC.
AUTO-IQ is a trademark of SharkNinja Operating LLC.

10   9   8   7   6

Printed in China.

TABLE OF CONTENTS

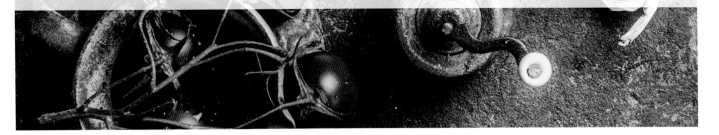

LOOKS LIKE A POT,
FEELS LIKE A JACKPOT

In today's go-go-go world, everyone's got a couple go-to recipes. But what if you had a hundred or more? And your taste buds were never bored? Imagine making full meals in minutes, in the same pot. Or perfectly poached eggs at the touch of a button. Or takeout favorites right at home. Now, stop imagining it and start cooking—thanks to the Ninja Cooking System with Auto-iQ™ Recipes, you win big at breakfast, lunch and dinner.

AUTO-IQ™ RECIPE PROGRAMS

Gone are the days of guessing in the kitchen. These four cooking modes do the thinking for you.

QUICK MEALS

All of these recipes are especially designed to get you in and out of the kitchen, quick and easy. Just add your ingredients and hit the button. All that's left to do is enjoy.

LAYERED BOWLS

These two-step recipes use the Auto-iQ Cooking System as a stovetop to sear proteins and build layers of flavor before cooking to perfection.

GRAINS

Cook grains such as oats and quinoa to the perfect consistency with the touch of a button.

POACHED INFUSIONS

Use this setting to poach fish, fruit, and more—like poached eggs for breakfast or shrimp cocktail for a classic dinner party appetizer.

MANUAL FUNCTIONS

These four functions make fundamental kitchen techniques easier and more convenient.

SLOW COOK

Worry-free ACCUTEMP temperature control operates behind the scenes to ensure your meals aren't overcooked or underdone, so you can slow cook with confidence.

BAKE

With a controllable range of temperatures from 250°–425°F, you can dry bake hearty roasts or steam bake breads, cakes, and more.

STEAM

Steam veggies for that delightful snap, or steam light proteins like seafood to play up their naturally subtle flavors.

STOVE TOP

An innovative heating element turns your Cooking System into a skillet so you can sear meats and sauté vegetables in one pot.

TRICKS OF THE TRADE

Here are a few tips to help you get the most out of your Auto-iQ™ Cooking System.

AT THE STORE

Organize your grocery list by the sections of your grocery store to make shopping a breeze.

Buy pre-cut vegetables when available to cut down on prep time.

PREPARE YOUR KITCHEN

Have the right tools on hand for prepping and measuring your ingredients. You will need both dry and liquid measuring cups (check out the next page to see why).

Designate a small container on your counter for trash-like package wrappings, vegetable trimmings, and used paper towels.

ALWAYS USE GOOD FORM

Familiarize yourself with the recipe by re-reading the ingredient list and directions.

Gather your ingredients, then measure and organize them by step.

Always use nonstick-safe utensils to avoid damaging the cooking pot's nonstick coating.

Meal need to be cooked a little longer? Simply set to BAKE DRY at 350° F for 5–10 minutes, checking for desired doneness.

DIETARY LABELS

 Gluten-Free

(DF) Dairy-Free

(VG) Vegetarian

(VE) Vegan

(PA) Paleo

 Adventurous Recipes

Adventurous Recipes let you take a bite on the wild side. Inspired by restaurant and takeout favorites from near and far, these recipes pack a ton of flavor into just one easy-to-follow Auto-iQ recipe.

MEASURING MATTERS

Dry and liquid measurements differ, so it's important to use the right tool for the job. Here's a simple breakdown of standard measuring cups for dry and liquid ingredients.

DRY MEASURING CUPS

Dry measuring cups are used to measure dry ingredients (like flour and sugar) as well as non-pourable wet ingredients (like peanut butter and sour cream).

LIQUID MEASURING CUPS

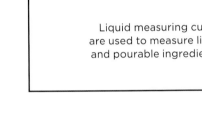

Liquid measuring cups are used to measure liquid and pourable ingredients.

Measuring Tip

Over a bowl, overfill the measuring cup. Then level the ingredient with a flat edge, like a butter knife or spatula. This will ensure an exact measurement and preserve the excess ingredient for future use.

Use dry measuring cups for:

- Flour
- Granulated white sugar
- Brown sugar
- Confectioners' sugar
- Oats & other grains
- Bread crumbs
- Cereal
- Peanut butter
- Sour cream
- Yogurt
- Cream cheese
- Fresh & frozen fruit

Measuring Tip

Place the measuring cup on your countertop before filling it. Once filled, bend down so you can see the measurement at eye level (looking at the cup from above will skew your view).

Use liquid measuring cups for:

- Water
- Oil
- Vinegar
- Milk
- Juice
- Stock/broth

AUTO-IQ KNOWS WHAT TO DO

Gone are the days of guessing in the kitchen. From hands-free grain preparation to delicately poached meals without the use of a stovetop, Auto-iQ does the thinking for you.

GO WITH THE GRAINS

GRAINS

Your Auto-iQ cooking system is now your sous chef, helping you quickly and easily make delicious side dishes and breakfasts such as quinoa and oats. Refer to the charts on the following pages, add your grain and liquid, and let the Auto-iQ program do the rest.

OLD-FASHIONED OATS

1 Place oats and liquid into the cooking pot, stir, and cover.

2 **Select Auto-iQ Grains: Recipe 1, 2, or 3 and press the START/STOP button.**

3 Stir and serve.

TIPS

For a flavorful variation, try using milk, almond milk, or coconut milk instead of water.

Stir in nuts and dried fruit at the end of the Auto-iQ program for added texture and flavor.

Stir in honey or maple syrup for added sweetness.

AUTO-IQ PROGRAM NUMBER	OATS	LIQUID*	COOK†	MAKES
1	1 cup	1 $3/4$ cups	13–18 minutes	4 servings
2	2 cups	3 $1/2$ cups	29–34 minutes	8 servings
3	3 cups	5 $1/4$ cups	27–32 minutes	12 servings

*Use the measurements in this chart instead of the measurements on your packaging.

†All cook times are estimates. Your Auto-iQ Cooking System will begin a countdown timer with five minutes left to cook.

STEEL-CUT OATS

1 Place oats and liquid into the cooking pot, stir, and cover.

2 Select Auto-iQ Grains: Recipe 4, 5, or 6 and press the START/STOP button.

3 Stir and serve.

NOTE: You may notice a little water left at the bottom of your pot when the cooking cycle is complete. You can either let this sit on "keep warm" or drain right away.

TIPS

For a flavorful variation, try using milk, almond milk, or coconut milk instead of water.

Stir in nuts and dried fruit at the end of the Auto-iQ program for added texture and flavor.

Stir in honey or maple syrup for added sweetness.

AUTO-IQ PROGRAM NUMBER	OATS	LIQUID*	COOK†	MAKES
4	1 cup	3 cups	55–60 minutes	4 servings
5	2 cups	6 cups	55–60 minutes	8 servings
6	3 cups	9 cups	72–77 minutes	12 servings

*Use the measurements in this chart instead of the measurements on your packaging.

†All cook times are estimates. Your Auto-iQ Cooking System will begin a countdown timer with five minutes left to cook.

QUINOA

1 Place quinoa and liquid into the cooking pot, stir, and cover.

2 Select Auto-iQ Grains: Recipe 7, 8, or 9 and press the START/STOP button.

3 Stir and serve.

TIPS

Quinoa is a protein-packed ancient grain that pairs well with poultry, makes salads heartier, and is a great base for grain bowls.

For a flavorful variation, try using stock instead of water.

AUTO-IQ PROGRAM NUMBER	QUINOA	LIQUID*	COOK†	MAKES
7	1 cup	2 cups	25–30 minutes	4 servings
8	2 cups	4 cups	35–40 minutes	8 servings
9	3 cups	6 cups	40–45 minutes	12 servings

*Use the measurements in this chart instead of the measurements on your packaging.

†All cook times are estimates. Your Auto-iQ Cooking System will begin a countdown timer with five minutes left to cook.

POACH PERFECT

POACHED INFUSIONS & STOCKS

Want delicate flavor that'll make your taste buds sing? Lightly poach everything from fish to eggs at the touch of a button (yes, really!). You can even experiment with different poaching liquids—like wines, milks, or stocks—to up the flavor ante.

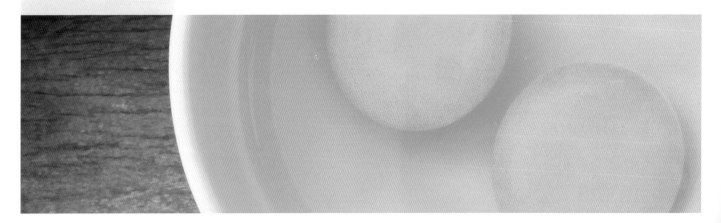

EGGS

1 Crack eggs into a single bowl.

2 Pour water into the cooking pot and cover. **Select Auto-iQ Poached Infusions: Recipe 1, 2, 3, or 4 and press the START/STOP button.** The water will start heating up to a gentle simmer.

3 At the first beep, which signifies the water has come to a simmer, the display will read "Add." Lift lid and pour eggs carefully into water. Cover pot and **press the START/STOP button.**

4 While eggs are poaching, line a plate with a paper towel and have a slotted spoon ready.

5 At the second beep, transfer eggs one by one with the slotted spoon onto the paper-towel-lined plate.

AUTO-IQ PROGRAM NUMBER	EGGS	WATER	PREP	COOK*	MAKES
1	2 large eggs	5 cups	2 minutes	16 1/2 minutes	1 serving
2	4 large eggs	5 cups	2 minutes	18 1/2 minutes	2 servings
3	6 large eggs	5 cups	2 minutes	18 1/2 minutes	3 servings
4	12 large eggs	5 cups	2 minutes	21 minutes	6 servings

TIPS

To help keep the egg whites from separating, add 1 tablespoon vinegar to the water.

Make Eggs Benedict, found on Page 98, with this process.

Crack your eggs first. This helps speed up the process and gives you more control over those delicate egg yolks, rather than cracking them right into the pot.

SHRIMP

(GF) (DF) (PA)

1 Pour liquid and any seasonings into the cooking pot and cover. **Select Auto-iQ Poached Infusions: Recipe 5 or 6 and press the START/STOP button.** The liquid will start heating up to a gentle simmer.

2 At the first beep, which signifies the liquid has come to a simmer, the display will read "Add." Lift lid and add shrimp carefully to liquid. Cover pot and **press the START/STOP button.**

3 While shrimp are poaching, place a colander in your sink.

4 At the second beep, CAREFULLY remove the cooking pot using oven mitts and drain shrimp in the colander.

5 Pat shrimp dry, then chill in refrigerator for 1–2 hours.

AUTO-IQ PROGRAM NUMBER	SHRIMP	LIQUID	PREP	COOK*	MAKES
5	1 pound uncooked **fresh** large shrimp, peeled, deveined	4 cups	10 minutes	19 minutes	8 servings
6	1 pound uncooked **frozen** large shrimp, peeled, deveined	4 cups	10 minutes	30 minutes	8 servings

FLAVOR INSPIRATION

Classic Shrimp Cocktail Seasonings

2 lemons, cut in half

10 peppercorns

1 tablespoon salt

2 bay leaves

TIPS

Mix it up by trying different poaching liquids like white wine, beer, or broth/stock.
- Use a dry white wine, like pinot grigio or sauvignon blanc. Use a 1-to-3 ratio of wine to water.
- Use a light beer, like a lager or ale. Use a 1-to-3 ratio of beer to water.

---

*All cook times are estimates. Your Auto-iQ Cooking System will begin a countdown timer with five minutes left to cook.

FISH

(GF) (DF) (PA)

1 Place all vegetables, liquids, and seasonings in the cooking pot and stir gently to incorporate.

2 Nestle the fish portions into the contents of the pot so they are roughly half submerged in the liquid and surrounded by aromatics and vegetables.

3 Cover pot and **select Auto-iQ Poached Infusions: Recipe 7, 8, or 9 and press the START/STOP button.**

AUTO-IQ PROGRAM NUMBER	FISH	LIQUID	PREP	COOK*	MAKES
7	2–6 uncooked fish pieces (4 ounces each, fish should have skin removed), $1/4$-inch to $1/2$-inch thick	4 cups	2–20 minutes	16 minutes	2–6 servings
8	2–6 uncooked fish pieces (4 ounces each), $3/4$-inch to 1-inch thick	4 cups	2–20 minutes	18 minutes	2–6 servings
9	2–6 uncooked fish pieces (4 ounces each), $1 1/4$-inches to $1 1/2$-inches thick	4 cups	2–20 minutes	20 minutes	2–6 servings

BEST FISH FOR POACHING

Best results are achieved with fish that is slightly thicker and heartier.

- Salmon
- Cod
- Grouper
- Halibut
- Arctic Char
- Steelhead Trout

FLAVOR INSPIRATION

Classic French Seasonings

3 cups water	2 bay leaves
1 cup white wine	4 sprigs parsley
1 lemon, cut in half, juiced	5 sprigs thyme
2 carrots, cut in quarters	3 cloves garlic, smashed
2 stalks celery, cut in quarters	1 tablespoon kosher salt
1 white onion, peeled, sliced	1 teaspoon peppercorns
1 leek, sliced	

Southeast Asian Seasonings

1 cup water	1 lime, zested, juiced
3 cups coconut milk	1 tablespoon fish sauce
1 lemongrass stem, smashed	1 tablespoon sesame oil
1-inch piece ginger, smashed	1 tablespoon sugar
3 cloves garlic, smashed	1 tablespoon kosher salt

Spicy Southwest Seasonings

4 cups water	1 tablespoon coriander seed
1 tablespoon paprika	1 tablespoon fennel seed
1 tablespoon ancho chili powder	1 orange, zested, juiced
2 dry chipotle peppers	1 tablespoon agave nectar
2 tablespoons cumin seed	

TIPS

Mix it up by trying different poaching liquids like red or white wine, broth/stock, or coconut milk.
- Use a dry white wine, like pinot grigio or sauvignon blanc. Use a 1-to-3 ratio of wine to water.
- Use a 3-to-1 ratio of coconut milk to water.

Make a reduction by straining the poaching liquid through a fine mesh sieve, discarding the vegetables and aromatics but reserving the liquid. Return liquid to pot, add 1/4 cup heavy cream, and cook on STOVE TOP HIGH for roughly 30 minutes, until the liquid has reduced by 75%. Turn unit off, and slowly whisk in 6 ounces cold butter cut into small cubes. Serve over your poached fish.

*All cook times are estimates. Your Auto-iQ Cooking System will begin a countdown timer with five minutes left to cook.

FRUIT

(GF) (VE) (PA)

1 Place liquid and seasonings in the cooking pot and stir gently to combine.

2 Add fruit, ensuring it is fully submerged in the liquid, cutting as needed.

3 Cover pot and **select Auto-iQ Poached Infusions: Recipe 10 and press the START/STOP button.**

4 At the beep, use a slotted spoon to remove the fruit from the poaching liquid.

AUTO-IQ PROGRAM NUMBER	FRUIT	LIQUID	PREP	COOK*	MAKES
10	1 pound fresh fruit, peeled, core or pit removed	6 cups	15 minutes	35 minutes	3 cups

BEST FRUIT FOR POACHING

Best results are found with modestly dense fresh fruit that are heartier.

- Pears
- Apples
- Plums
- Cherries
- Peaches
- Pineapple

FLAVOR INSPIRATION

Warm Spice Seasonings

4 cups dry white wine

2 cups water or apple cider

3 cups sugar

½ teaspoon vanilla extract

2 cinnamon sticks

4 whole cloves

Savory Seasonings

4 cups red wine

2 cups water

2 cups sugar

1 cup molasses

2 teaspoons fennel seed

1 teaspoon peppercorns

2 sprigs rosemary

4 sprigs thyme

Citrus Seasonings

4 cups orange juice

2 cups water

1 cup sugar

1 cup honey

zest and juice of 2 lemons

2 teaspoons coriander seed

2 whole star anise

TIPS

For best results, peel and core or pit your fruit before cutting it into 1"-3" chunks or slices so fruit is fully submerged in liquid.

Mix it up by trying different poaching liquids, like wine, juice, or cider. Use a 2-to-1 ratio of wine, juice, or cider to water to not overwhelm your fruit.

Make a reduction by straining the poaching liquid through a fine mesh sieve. Return liquid to pot and cook on STOVE TOP HIGH for roughly 45 minutes, until liquid has reduced by 75% and has a texture similar to caramel sauce. Spoon over poached fruit, ice cream, yogurt, or granola.

*All cook times are estimates. Your Auto-iQ Cooking System will begin a countdown timer with five minutes left to cook.

Questions? 1-877-646-5288 | ninjakitchen.com   25

STOCKS

(GF) (DF) (PA)

1 Place all the ingredients in the cooking pot and cover. **Select Auto-iQ Poached Infusions: Recipe 11 or 12 and press the START/STOP button.**

2 Place colander over a large bowl.

3 At the beep, CAREFULLY remove the cooking pot using oven mitts and drain stock in the colander.

4 Allow stock to cool, uncovered, at room temperature. When cool, skim any fat from the surface of the strained stock and discard. Use immediately, or cover and store in the refrigerator up to 1 week or in the freezer up to 6 months.

AUTO-IQ PROGRAM NUMBER	STOCK	LIQUID	PREP	COOK*	MAKES
11	Chicken Stock	10 cups	15 minutes	3 1/2 hours	10 cups
12	Vegetable Stock	10 cups	15 minutes	68 minutes	10 cups

ENHANCE THE FLAVOR

Before starting your stock, sear bones and/or sauté vegetables on STOVE TOP HIGH until browned.

STOCK INSPIRATION

Chicken Stock

2 pounds chicken bones

1/2 pound carrots, peeled, cut in half

1/2 pound celery, cut in quarters

1 pound onions, peeled, cut in quarters

1 tablespoon tomato paste

1/2 cup fresh herbs such as parsley, thyme, bay leaves, and/or rosemary

1 tablespoon peppercorns

Vegetable Stock

1 pound onions, peeled, cut in quarters

1/2 pound carrots, peeled, cut in quarters

1/2 pound celery, cut in quarters

1/2 cup fresh herbs such as parsley, thyme, bay leaves, and/or rosemary

TIPS

Don't add salt. This allows you to better season your dishes when using your stock later.

For even more flavor, generously season with other aromatics such as fennel or coriander seed.

Save your leftover vegetables throughout the week and use them when making your stock.

For sauces and soups on the fly, keep your stock in a sealed container in the refrigerator up to 1 week, or freeze it in ice cube trays, transfer to freezer bags, and store frozen up to 6 months.

*All cook times are estimates. Your Auto-iQ Cooking System will begin a countdown timer with five minutes left to cook.

Questions? 1-877-646-5288 | ninjakitchen.com   27

THESE ONLY TASTE LIKE THEY TOOK HOURS

QUICK MEALS

We're all pretty strapped for time when it comes to cooking at home. But the Auto-iQ Cooking System is set up to do the work for you—just select a pre-set recipe, add your ingredients and hit a button. All you have to do is enjoy.

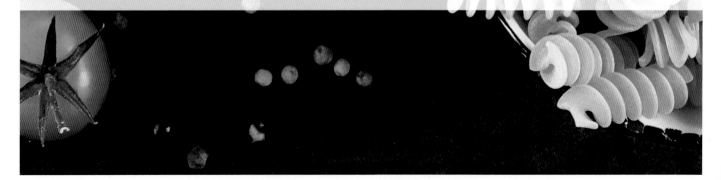

BREAKFAST

Herb Frittata	30
Red Pepper & Potato Frittata	31
Rolled Oats with Peaches, Honey & Walnuts	31
Banana Nut Steel-Cut Oatmeal	33
Cinnamon Roll Breakfast Casserole	33

BEEF

Quick Beef Chili	34
Asian Meatballs with Broccoli	34
Green Chili & Chorizo Grits	35
Meat Ravioli with Marinara	35
Franks & Beans	36
Pepperoni Pizza Mac & Cheese	37
Spiced Ground Beef with Polenta	37

POULTRY

Chicken Spinach Noodle Bake	39
Chicken Spinach Artichoke Casserole	39
BBQ Chicken Dinner	40
Coconut Chicken Curry Stew	40
Green Chile Chicken Enchiladas	41
Chicken Tikka Masala	42
Chicken Corn Casserole	42
Turkey Lasagna	44
Chicken Curry	45
Thai Coconut Stew	45
Sweet Chili Chicken	47

SEAFOOD

Salmon & Broccoli Slaw	48
Ginger Shrimp & Green Beans	48
Lobster Ravioli in Vodka Sauce	49
Thai Mussels	50
White Wine Mussels	50

VEGETARIAN

Cheese Tortellini with Pesto	51
Baked Vegetable Polenta	52
Mexican Bean Casserole	52
Chickpea Curry	53
Vegetarian Tortilla Soup	54
Asian Pot Sticker Soup	55
Vegetable Pad Thai	55
Pinto Bean & Vegetable Enchilada Casserole	56
Tofu Lentil Stew	56
Pierogi with Horseradish Sauce	57
Cuban-Style Black Beans	57

Meal need to be cooked a little longer? Simply set to BAKE DRY at 350°F for 5–10 minutes, checking for desired doneness.

RECIPE
1

HERB FRITTATA

GF VG

PREP: 15 MINUTES | **COOK:** 20 MINUTES | **MAKES:** 4–6 SERVINGS

INGREDIENTS

10 large eggs, beaten

$2/3$ cup whole milk

1 cup fresh parsley, chopped

1 cup fresh basil leaves, chopped

2 tablespoons fresh chives, chopped

1 cup cherry tomatoes or grape tomatoes

$1/4$ teaspoon salt

$1/4$ teaspoon pepper

1 cup crumbled feta cheese

DIRECTIONS

1 Grease pot or coat with canola spray. Place all ingredients, except feta, into the pot, and gently stir to combine. Sprinkle feta on top, then cover pot.

2 Select Auto-iQ Quick Meals: Recipe 1 and press the START/STOP button.

SWAP

Gruyere cheese for feta cheese

Tip: Serve with multigrain toast or a simple green salad.

RECIPE 2

RED PEPPER & POTATO FRITTATA

PREP: 10 MINUTES | **COOK:** 29 MINUTES | **MAKES:** 6-8 SERVINGS

INGREDIENTS

10 large eggs

3 tablespoons olive oil

1 teaspoon kosher salt

1/2 teaspoon ground black pepper

1/3 package (about 8 ounces) frozen shredded hash brown potatoes

1 medium onion, peeled, diced

2 red bell peppers, diced

DIRECTIONS

1 In a mixing bowl, whisk together eggs, olive oil, salt, and black pepper.

2 Place hash browns, onion, peppers, and egg mixture into the pot. Gently stir to combine, then cover pot.

3 Select Auto-iQ Quick Meals: Recipe 2 and press the START/STOP button.

Tip: Serve warm for breakfast or cold, cut out into small pieces, as tapas for a party.

RECIPE 3

ROLLED OATS WITH PEACHES, HONEY & WALNUTS

PREP: 15 MINUTES | **COOK:** 22 MINUTES | **MAKES:** 4 SERVINGS

INGREDIENTS

2 1/3 cups water

1 bag (16 ounces) frozen peach slices

1 cup uncooked old-fashioned whole grain rolled oats

2/3 cup chopped walnuts

1/2 teaspoon vanilla extract

1/4 teaspoon ground cinnamon

1/4 teaspoon kosher salt

OPTIONAL

1/4 cup milk, for serving

1/4 cup honey, for serving

DIRECTIONS

1 Place all ingredients into the pot. Stir to combine, then cover pot.

2 Select Auto-iQ Quick Meals: Recipe 3 and press the START/STOP button.

3 Stir and serve.

SWAPS

Frozen mixed berries for peaches

Sliced almonds for walnuts

Maple syrup for honey

Meal need to be cooked a little longer? Simply set to BAKE DRY at 350°F for 5–10 minutes, checking for desired doneness.

BANANA NUT STEEL-CUT OATMEAL

RECIPE
4

BANANA NUT STEEL-CUT OATMEAL

(GF) (VG)

PREP: 15 MINUTES | **COOK:** 25 MINUTES | **MAKES:** 4 SERVINGS

INGREDIENTS

3 3/4 cups water

1 cup uncooked
steel-cut oats

1/2 cup chopped walnuts

1 tablespoon flaxseed

1/2 teaspoon
vanilla extract

1/4 teaspoon
ground cinnamon

3/4 cup dried fruit,
like cherries or raisins

1/4 teaspoon kosher salt

OPTIONAL

*3 tablespoons light
brown sugar, for serving*

*2 ripe bananas,
sliced, for serving*

*1/4 cup low-fat milk,
for serving*

DIRECTIONS

1 Place all ingredients into the pot. Do not cover.

2 Select Auto-iQ Quick Meals: Recipe 4 and press
the START/STOP button.

3 Stir and serve.

RECIPE
5

CINNAMON ROLL BREAKFAST CASSEROLE

(VG)

PREP: 10 MINUTES | **COOK:** 25 MINUTES | **MAKES:** 8 SERVINGS

INGREDIENTS

5 large eggs

2/3 cup milk

1/2 cup heavy cream

1/4 cup sugar

1 teaspoon
vanilla extract

1/4 teaspoon
ground cinnamon

1/4 teaspoon kosher salt

4 large cooked
cinnamon rolls,
cut in 1-inch chunks

1/2 package (4 ounces)
cream cheese, cut in
1/2-inch pieces

DIRECTIONS

1 Lightly grease pot. In a mixing bowl, whisk together
eggs, milk, heavy cream, sugar, vanilla, cinnamon,
and salt.

2 Place cinnamon roll chunks, cream cheese, and egg
mixture into the pot, then cover.

3 Select Auto-iQ Quick Meals: Recipe 5 and press
the START/STOP button.

Meal need to be cooked a little longer? Simply set to BAKE DRY
at 350°F for 5–10 minutes, checking for desired doneness.

RECIPE 6

QUICK BEEF CHILI

PREP: 10 MINUTES | **COOK:** 30 MINUTES | **MAKES:** 4-6 SERVINGS

(GF) (DF)

INGREDIENTS

1 ½ pounds uncooked
ground beef

1 can (28 ounces)
diced tomatoes

1 can (15 ounces) kidney
beans, rinsed, drained

1 large green bell
pepper, chopped

1 large onion,
peeled, chopped

2 tablespoons
chili powder

½ teaspoon
ground cumin

1 teaspoon salt

DIRECTIONS

1 Place beef in pot and break apart with a spatula.

2 Place remaining ingredients in pot. Stir to combine,
then cover pot.

3 Select Auto-iQ Quick Meals: Recipe 6 and press
the START/STOP button.

4 Stir and serve.

SWAPS

Ground chicken or ground turkey for ground beef

Black beans for kidney beans

*Tip: Serve with your favorite toppings such
as diced avocado, sliced scallions, and grated
cheddar cheese.*

RECIPE 7

ASIAN MEATBALLS
WITH BROCCOLI

PREP: 5 MINUTES | **COOK:** 25 MINUTES | **MAKES:** 4 SERVINGS

(DF)

INGREDIENTS

½ package (12 ounces)
frozen mini beef
meatballs

1 pound frozen
broccoli florets

½ cup low-sodium
beef broth

½ cup hoisin sauce

3 tablespoons
low-sodium soy sauce

2 tablespoons
rice vinegar

1 tablespoon light
brown sugar

½ teaspoon
garlic powder

¼ teaspoon
ground ginger

DIRECTIONS

1 Place all ingredients into the pot. Stir to combine,
then cover pot.

2 Select Auto-iQ Quick Meals: Recipe 7 and press
the START/START button.

3 Stir and serve.

SWAPS

Turkey meatballs for beef meatballs

Brussels sprouts, cut in half, for broccoli florets

RECIPE 8

GREEN CHILE & CHORIZO GRITS (GF) (DF)

PREP: 10 MINUTES | **COOK:** 25 MINUTES | **MAKES:** 6 SERVINGS

INGREDIENTS

1 cup old-fashioned grits

3 cups water

1 can (10 ounces) diced tomatoes and green chilies

2 cans (4 ounces each) diced green chiles

1/2 package (6 ounces) cooked chorizo, chopped

1/2 teaspoon ground black pepper

1/4 teaspoon kosher salt

OPTIONAL
1 cup shredded Colby-Jack cheese, for serving

1/4 cup fresh cilantro, chopped, for serving

DIRECTIONS

1 Place all ingredients into the pot. Stir to combine, then cover pot.

2 Select Auto-iQ Quick Meals: Recipe 8 and press the START/STOP button.

3 Stir and serve.

SWAPS

Corn grits for old-fashioned grits

Andouille chicken sausage for chorizo

RECIPE 9

MEAT RAVIOLI WITH MARINARA

PREP: 5 MINUTES | **COOK:** 25 MINUTES | **MAKES:** 6 SERVINGS

INGREDIENTS

2 pounds frozen meat ravioli

1 jar (24 ounces) marinara sauce

1 2/3 cups water

1 teaspoon Italian seasoning

1/4 teaspoon ground black pepper

1/4 teaspoon garlic powder

OPTIONAL
1/4 cup fresh basil, chopped, for serving

Grated Parmesan cheese, for serving

DIRECTIONS

1 Place all ingredients into the pot. Stir to combine, then cover pot.

2 Select Auto-iQ Quick Meals: Recipe 9 and press the START/START button.

3 Stir and serve.

SWAPS

Cheese ravioli for meat ravioli

Vodka sauce or Alfredo sauce for marinara sauce

Meal need to be cooked a little longer? Simply set to BAKE DRY at 350°F for 5-10 minutes, checking for desired doneness.

RECIPE
10

FRANKS & BEANS

(GF) (DF)

PREP: 10 MINUTES | **COOK:** 30 MINUTES | **MAKES:** 6 SERVINGS

INGREDIENTS

3 cans (15 ounces each) cannellini beans, rinsed, drained

4 hot dogs, cut in 1-inch pieces

1 onion, peeled, minced

1 cup lightly packed brown sugar

1 cup ketchup

$3/4$ cup water

$1/3$ cup molasses

$1/4$ cup apple cider vinegar

1 tablespoon dry mustard

DIRECTIONS

1 Place all ingredients into the pot. Stir to combine, then cover pot.

2 Select Auto-iQ Quick Meals: Recipe 10 and press the START/STOP button.

3 Stir and serve.

SWAPS

Baked beans for cannellini beans

Cooked sausage for hot dogs

Tip: *You can replace the molasses, brown sugar, vinegar, and ketchup with some BBQ sauce.*

RECIPE 11

PEPPERONI PIZZA MAC & CHEESE

PREP: 5 MINUTES | **COOK:** 25 MINUTES | **MAKES:** 6-8 SERVINGS

INGREDIENTS

5 cups water

1 jar (14 ounces)
pizza sauce

1 package (8 ounces)
cream cheese, softened,
cut in 1-inch pieces

1 pound uncooked
mini wheel pasta

1 bag (4 ounces)
mini pepperoni

1 teaspoon Italian
seasoning

1/2 teaspoon crushed
red pepper

3 cups shredded
mozzarella cheese,
for serving

DIRECTIONS

1 Place all ingredients, except mozzarella, into the
pot. Stir to combine, then cover pot.

2 **Select Auto-iQ Quick Meals: Recipe 11 and press
the START/STOP button.**

3 Add cheese. Stir and serve.

SWAPS

Elbow pasta for mini wheel pasta

Turkey pepperoni or diced cooked chicken sausage
for pepperoni

> *Tip:* For a loaded version, add 1/4 cup each
> sliced black olives and canned quartered
> artichoke hearts.

RECIPE 12

SPICED GROUND BEEF WITH POLENTA

PREP: 10 MINUTES | **COOK:** 25 MINUTES | **MAKES:** 4-6 SERVINGS

INGREDIENTS

2 pounds uncooked
lean ground beef

1 tablespoon
chili powder

1 teaspoon paprika

1 teaspoon salt

1/2 teaspoon
ground cumin

1/4 teaspoon crushed
red pepper

1 can (15 ounces)
tomato sauce

1 log (18 ounces)
cooked polenta,
cut in 1/2-inch rounds
(about 12-14 total)

DIRECTIONS

1 Place all ingredients, except polenta, into the pot.
Stir to combine, making sure to break up any large
chunks of beef.

2 Place polenta on top of beef mixture, then cover pot.

3 **Select Auto-iQ Quick Meals: Recipe 12 and press
the START/STOP button.**

SWAPS

Ground turkey for ground beef

1 cup frozen corn for polenta

> *Tip:* For extra protein, stir in a can of rinsed and
> drained black beans before topping with polenta.

Meal need to be cooked a little longer? Simply set to BAKE DRY
at 350°F for 5-10 minutes, checking for desired doneness.

CHICKEN SPINACH NOODLE BAKE

RECIPE 13

CHICKEN SPINACH NOODLE BAKE

PREP: 10 MINUTES | **COOK:** 30 MINUTES | **MAKES:** 6 SERVINGS

INGREDIENTS

1 1/2 pounds uncooked boneless, skinless chicken breasts, cubed

3 1/2 cups water

1 pound uncooked elbow pasta

1 pound whole-milk ricotta cheese

1 1/2 cups shredded mozzarella cheese

3 cloves garlic, peeled, minced

4 cups fresh baby spinach

1 teaspoon salt

DIRECTIONS

1 Place all ingredients into the pot. Stir to combine, then cover pot.

2 Select Auto-iQ Quick Meals: Recipe 13 and press the START/STOP button.

3 Serve immediately.

SWAPS

Cavatappi or cavatelli pasta for elbow pasta

Swiss chard or kale for spinach

RECIPE 14

CHICKEN SPINACH ARTICHOKE CASSEROLE

PREP: 15 MINUTES | **COOK:** 25 MINUTES | **MAKES:** 4–6 SERVINGS

INGREDIENTS

1 rotisserie chicken (2.5–3 pounds), meat shredded

2 boxes (10 ounces each) chopped spinach, thawed, squeezed of excess liquid

3 cans (14 ounces each) quartered artichoke hearts, drained

1 bunch scallions, chopped

1 package (8 ounces) fresh mozzarella cheese, shredded

1/2 cup grated Parmesan cheese, plus more for serving

1 cup heavy cream

1 teaspoon salt

DIRECTIONS

1 Place all ingredients into the pot and stir to combine, then cover pot.

2 Select Auto-iQ Quick Meals: Recipe 14 and press the START/STOP button.

3 Sprinkle with additional Parmesan and serve.

SWAPS

Leftover turkey for rotisserie chicken

Whole milk or full-fat coconut milk for heavy cream

Meal need to be cooked a little longer? Simply set to BAKE DRY at 350°F for 5-10 minutes, checking for desired doneness.

RECIPE 15 BBQ CHICKEN DINNER

PREP: 5 MINUTES | **COOK:** 25 MINUTES | **MAKES:** 4-6 SERVINGS

INGREDIENTS

2 pounds uncooked
boneless, skinless
chicken thighs,
cut in half

1 medium onion, peeled,
thinly sliced

1 cup barbecue sauce

1 can (28 ounces)
baked beans

DIRECTIONS

1 Place all ingredients into the pot. Stir to combine, then cover pot.

2 Select Auto-iQ Quick Meals: Recipe 15 and press the START/STOP button.

SWAP

Boneless pork chops for chicken thighs

Tip: Serve on rice with corn on the cob and coleslaw for a complete Fourth of July meal.

RECIPE 16 COCONUT CHICKEN CURRY STEW

PREP: 10 MINUTES | **COOK:** 20 MINUTES | **MAKES:** 4-6 SERVINGS

INGREDIENTS

2 ½ pounds uncooked
boneless, skinless
chicken breasts,
cut in 1-inch pieces

2 cups fresh snow peas

1 can (13.66 ounces)
coconut milk

3-inch piece
lemongrass, minced

2 cloves garlic,
peeled, minced

2 ½ tablespoons
curry powder

1 tablespoon sugar

1 tablespoon grated
fresh ginger

¼ teaspoon crushed
red pepper

OPTIONAL

*1 cup toasted
sweetened coconut
flakes, for serving*

*½ cup fresh cilantro,
chopped, for serving*

DIRECTIONS

1 Place all ingredients into the pot. Stir to combine, then cover pot.

2 Select Auto-iQ Quick Meals: Recipe 16 and press the START/STOP button.

3 Stir and serve.

SWAPS

Firm tofu for chicken breasts

Green bell peppers for snow peas

Juice and zest of 1 lime for lemongrass

GREEN CHILE CHICKEN ENCHILADAS

PREP: 10 MINUTES | **COOK:** 20 MINUTES | **MAKES:** 4 SERVINGS

INGREDIENTS

3 cups shredded
chicken

1 package (8 ounces)
cream cheese, softened

$1/2$ cup sour cream

$1/2$ cup fresh cilantro,
chopped

1 can (4.5 ounces)
chopped green chiles

$1/2$ teaspoon
garlic powder

1 teaspoon
ground cumin

$1/2$ teaspoon salt

1 can (28 ounces)
red or green enchilada
sauce, divided

18 (6-inch) corn
tortillas, divided

1 package (16 ounces)
shredded Monterey Jack
cheese, divided

OPTIONAL
*1 tablespoon cilantro,
chopped, for serving*

DIRECTIONS

1 Stir together the chicken, cream cheese, sour
cream, cilantro, green chiles, and spices in a bowl;
set aside.

2 Pour 1 cup enchilada sauce into the pot. Arrange
6 tortillas in a single layer in pot, slightly overlapping.

3 Evenly cover tortillas with half the chicken mixture,
1 ¼ cups cheese, and ½ cup enchilada sauce. Place
6 tortillas on top and repeat process.

4 Arrange remaining tortillas on top and cover with
1 ½ cups sauce. Sprinkle with remaining cheese and
cover pot.

5 Select Auto-iQ Quick Meals: Recipe 17 and press
the START/STOP button.

Meal need to be cooked a little longer? Simply set to BAKE DRY
at 350°F for 5–10 minutes, checking for desired doneness.

RECIPE 18

CHICKEN TIKKA MASALA

PREP: 15 MINUTES | **COOK:** 30 MINUTES | **MAKES:** 4-6 SERVINGS

INGREDIENTS

2 pounds uncooked boneless, skinless chicken breasts, cut in 1-inch chunks

1 can (28 ounces) crushed tomatoes

1 pound frozen peas

1 onion, peeled, chopped

3 cloves garlic, peeled, chopped

1-inch piece fresh ginger, peeled, minced

1 tablespoon ground garam masala seasoning

1 1/2 teaspoons salt

1 teaspoon ground turmeric

3/4 cup heavy cream

DIRECTIONS

1 Place all ingredients into the pot and stir to combine, then cover pot.

2 Select Auto-iQ Quick Meals: Recipe 18 and press the START/STOP button.

3 Stir and serve.

SWAPS

Chicken thighs for chicken breasts

Coconut cream for heavy cream

Tip: Serve with rice or naan on the side. Garnish with chopped cilantro, if desired.

RECIPE 19

CHICKEN CORN CASSEROLE

PREP: 10 MINUTES | **COOK:** 15 MINUTES | **MAKES:** 4 SERVINGS

INGREDIENTS

1 rotisserie chicken (3 pounds), shredded (about 5 cups shredded chicken)

1 can (15.5 ounces) corn, drained

1 can (10.5 ounces) condensed cream of chicken soup

1 cup sour cream

1 1/2 cups butter crackers, roughly crushed, divided

DIRECTIONS

1 Place chicken, corn, soup, sour cream, and 3/4 cup crackers into the pot. Stir to combine, then cover pot.

2 Select Auto-iQ Quick Meals: Recipe 19 and press the START/STOP button.

3 Top with remaining crackers and serve.

SWAPS

Cream of mushroom soup or cream of celery soup for cream of chicken soup

Greek yogurt for sour cream

Tip: Serve with a green salad for a simple supper.

Meal need to be cooked a little longer? Simply set to BAKE DRY at 350°F for 5-10 minutes, checking for desired doneness.

CHICKEN TIKKA MASALA

TURKEY LASAGNA

PREP: 10 MINUTES | **COOK:** 30 MINUTES | **MAKES:** 4–6 SERVINGS

INGREDIENTS

1 pound uncooked ground turkey (preferably dark meat)

1 jar (24 ounces) marinara sauce, divided

8 uncooked no-boil lasagna pasta sheets, divided

1 medium zucchini, cut in 1/4-inch thick rounds

1 pound whole-milk ricotta cheese

1 1/2 cups shredded mozzarella cheese, divided

DIRECTIONS

1 Place turkey and 1/3 cup sauce into the pot. Cover with 4 sheets pasta, breaking up the fourth to cover the sides of the pan.

2 Scatter the zucchini slices over the pasta. Spread with ricotta and sprinkle with 1 cup mozzarella cheese. Cover with half the remaining sauce.

3 Layer the remaining pasta, then top with the remaining sauce and mozzarella cheese. Cover pot.

4 Select Auto-iQ Quick Meals: Recipe 20 and press the START/STOP button.

5 For best results, let stand 5 to 10 minutes before serving.

SWAPS

Ground beef or ground chicken for ground turkey

Eggplant for zucchini

RECIPE 21

CHICKEN CURRY

(GF) (DF)

PREP: 15 MINUTES | **COOK:** 30 MINUTES | **MAKES:** 4–6 SERVINGS

INGREDIENTS

1 1/2 pounds uncooked boneless, skinless chicken breasts, cut in 1-inch strips

1 onion, peeled, sliced

2 cloves garlic, peeled, chopped

1 red bell pepper, sliced

1 1/2 tablespoons curry powder

2 tablespoons honey

1 can (15 ounces) diced tomatoes

1/2 cup chicken stock

1/2 cup full-fat coconut milk

1 1/2 teaspoons salt

DIRECTIONS

1 Place all ingredients into the pot. Stir to combine, then cover pot.

2 Select Auto-iQ Quick Meals: Recipe 21 and press the START/STOP button.

SWAPS

Heavy cream for coconut milk

Agave nectar for honey

Tip: Serve with white or brown rice. Garnish with chopped cilantro, if desired.

RECIPE 22

THAI COCONUT STEW

(DF) (A)

PREP: 10 MINUTES | **COOK:** 30 MINUTES | **MAKES:** 4 SERVINGS

INGREDIENTS

1 can (14 ounces) coconut milk

2 tablespoons lime juice

2 tablespoons lemongrass, minced

2 cups uncooked jasmine rice

1 tablespoon salt

1 teaspoon ground black pepper

1 pound uncooked boneless, skinless chicken breasts, cut in 1-inch pieces

4 cups chicken stock

1 pint (6 ounces) button mushrooms, sliced

2 tablespoons fresh ginger, minced

3 cups water

OPTIONAL

1/4 cup fresh cilantro, chopped, for serving

DIRECTIONS

1 Place all ingredients into the pot. Stir to combine, and cover pot.

2 Select Auto-iQ Quick Meals: Recipe 22 and press the START/STOP button.

3 Stir and serve.

SWAP

White basmati rice for jasmine rice

Meal need to be cooked a little longer? Simply set to BAKE DRY at 350°F for 5–10 minutes, checking for desired doneness.

SWEET CHILI CHICKEN

RECIPE
23

SWEET CHILI CHICKEN

(DF)

PREP: 15 MINUTES | **COOK:** 25 MINUTES | **MAKES:** 2-4 SERVINGS

INGREDIENTS

1 pound uncooked
chicken tenderloins

1 red bell pepper,
cut in 1-inch pieces

2 cups (about 6 ounces)
snow peas, trimmed

1 cup pineapple chunks,
fresh or canned, drained

1/4 cup sweet chili sauce

2 tablespoons
low-sodium soy sauce

OPTIONAL

*1/3 cup roasted or
candied cashews,
chopped, for serving*

DIRECTIONS

1 Place all ingredients into the pot. Stir to combine,
then cover pot.

2 **Select Auto-iQ Quick Meals: Recipe 23 and press
the START/STOP button.**

3 Stir and serve.

SWAPS

Chicken breasts for chicken tenderloins

Frozen peas for snow peas

Any unsalted roasted nuts for cashews

*Tip: For a heartier meal, serve over brown rice,
white rice, or rice noodles.*

Meal need to be cooked a little longer? Simply set to BAKE DRY
at 350°F for 5-10 minutes, checking for desired doneness.

RECIPE 24
SALMON & BROCCOLI SLAW

PREP: 20 MINUTES | **COOK:** 23 MINUTES | **MAKES:** 4 SERVINGS

INGREDIENTS

1 bag (12 ounces) broccoli slaw

1 shallot, peeled, minced

5 cloves garlic, peeled, minced

1 teaspoon ground cumin, divided

1 tablespoon paprika, divided

1 tablespoon dry mustard, divided

2 pounds uncooked salmon fillets, cut in quarters

1 tablespoon salt

1 teaspoon ground black pepper

3 cups water

1 1/2 cups uncooked Israeli couscous

OPTIONAL

1 tablespoon chives, minced, for serving

DIRECTIONS

1 Mix broccoli slaw with shallot, garlic, ½ teaspoon cumin, ½ tablespoon paprika, and ½ tablespoon dry mustard.

2 Season salmon with remaining spices, salt, and pepper. Add water, couscous, and seasoned vegetables to the pot. Next, add the salmon and cover the pot.

3 Select Auto-iQ Quick Meals: Recipe 24 and press the START/STOP button.

SWAPS

1 bag (14 ounces) coleslaw mix for broccoli slaw

Orzo for Israeli couscous

RECIPE 25
GINGER SHRIMP & GREEN BEANS

PREP: 15 MINUTES | **COOK:** 18 MINUTES | **MAKES:** 2–4 SERVINGS

INGREDIENTS

1 pound uncooked large shrimp (16-18 count), peeled, deveined

1 package (8 ounces) green beans, trimmed

2-inch piece fresh ginger, peeled, minced

2 cloves garlic, peeled, minced

1 can (8 ounces) sliced water chestnuts, drained

1/3 cup chicken stock

1 tablespoon low-sodium soy sauce

1 tablespoon mirin

1 tablespoon toasted sesame oil

DIRECTIONS

1 Place all ingredients into the pot. Stir to combine, then cover pot.

2 Select Auto-iQ Quick Meals: Recipe 25 and press the START/STOP button.

3 Serve immediately.

SWAPS

Tofu for shrimp

Baby corn for water chestnuts

Rice wine for mirin

Tip: For a heartier meal, serve over steamed white or brown rice.

LOBSTER RAVIOLI IN VODKA SAUCE (A)

PREP: 10 MINUTES | **COOK:** 25 MINUTES | **MAKES:** 6 SERVINGS

INGREDIENTS

2 pounds frozen
lobster ravioli

1 jar (24 ounces)
vodka sauce

1 3/4 cups water

1 teaspoon garlic powder

2 tablespoons fresh
tarragon, chopped

1/4 teaspoon crushed
red pepper

OPTIONAL
*1/3 cup grated Parmesan
cheese, for serving*

DIRECTIONS

1 Place all ingredients into the pot, then cover pot.

2 **Select Auto-iQ Quick Meals: Recipe 26 and press
   the START/STOP button.**

3 Stir and serve.

SWAPS

Cheese or mushroom ravioli for lobster ravioli

Basil for tarragon

Meal need to be cooked a little longer? Simply set to BAKE DRY
at 350°F for 5–10 minutes, checking for desired doneness.

**RECIPE
27**

THAI MUSSELS

PREP: 15 MINUTES | **COOK:** 30 MINUTES | **MAKES:** 6 SERVINGS

INGREDIENTS

3 pounds fresh mussels, rinsed, debearded

1 can (14 ounces) full-fat coconut milk

Zest and juice of 4 limes

2 tablespoons lemongrass, minced

2 tablespoons ginger, minced

1 tablespoon salt

4 cups water

1/2 package (8 ounces) uncooked linguine, broken in half

2 tablespoons red curry paste

1 pound sugar snap peas

1 tablespoon fish sauce

DIRECTIONS

1 Place all ingredients into the pot. Stir to combine, then cover pot.

2 Select Auto-iQ Quick Meals: Recipe 27 and press the START/STOP button.

3 Serve immediately.

SWAPS

Littleneck clams for mussels

White or rice vinegar for fish sauce

Tip: Garnish with any combination of chopped cilantro, basil, and mint.

**RECIPE
28**

WHITE WINE MUSSELS

PREP: 10 MINUTES | **COOK:** 25 MINUTES | **MAKES:** 2 SERVINGS

INGREDIENTS

3/4 box (12 ounces) uncooked angel hair pasta

5 cloves garlic, peeled, minced

1 small bunch fresh parsley, chopped (about 1/2 cup)

1 1/2 cups dry white wine

1 cup water

3 tablespoons butter, cut in pieces

2 1/2 pounds uncooked mussels, scrubbed, rinsed

DIRECTIONS

1 Place all ingredients, except mussels, into the pot and stir to combine.

2 Add the mussels, then cover pot.

3 Select Auto-iQ Quick Meals: Recipe 28 and press the START/STOP button.

4 Stir and serve.

SWAP

Littleneck clams for mussels

Tip: Pinot grigio or sauvignon blanc wine would work well in this recipe.

RECIPE
29

CHEESE TORTELLINI WITH PESTO (VG)

PREP: 5 MINUTES | **COOK:** 20 MINUTES | **MAKES:** 6 SERVINGS

INGREDIENTS

2 pounds frozen cheese tortellini

2 cups low-sodium vegetable broth

3/4 cup basil pesto

1/2 cup sundried tomatoes, chopped

1/3 cup water

1/2 teaspoon ground black pepper

OPTIONAL
Grated asiago cheese, for serving

DIRECTIONS

1 Place all ingredients into the pot. Stir to combine, then cover pot.

2 Select Auto-iQ Quick Meals: Recipe 29 and press the START/STOP button.

3 Stir and serve.

SWAP

Frozen mini ravioli for cheese tortellini

Tip: Add chopped prosciutto and pine nuts for a northern Italian twist.

Meal need to be cooked a little longer? Simply set to BAKE DRY at 350°F for 5–10 minutes, checking for desired doneness.

BAKED VEGETABLE POLENTA  (GF) (VG)

PREP: 10 MINUTES | **COOK:** 30 MINUTES | **MAKES:** 4 SERVINGS

INGREDIENTS

2 tablespoons extra virgin olive oil

1 large red onion, peeled, cut in 1/4-inch rounds

1 medium yellow squash, cut in 1/4-inch rounds

1 medium zucchini, cut in 1/4-inch rounds

1 1/2 pounds vine-ripened tomatoes (about 4 medium tomatoes), cut in 1/4-inch rounds

Salt and pepper, to taste

1 log (18 ounces) cooked polenta, cut in 1/4-inch rounds (about 12–14 total)

1/4 cup grated Parmesan cheese

DIRECTIONS

1 Pour the olive oil into the pot. Layer the onion, summer squash, zucchini, and then the tomatoes on top of oil. Season generously with salt and pepper.

2 Layer the polenta on top. Sprinkle with Parmesan cheese, then cover pot.

3 Select Auto-iQ Quick Meals: Recipe 30 and press the START/STOP button.

SWAPS

1 can (15 ounces) whole tomatoes for vine-ipened tomatoes

1 cup frozen corn for polenta

MEXICAN BEAN CASSEROLE (GF) (DF) (VG)

PREP: 10 MINUTES | **COOK:** 25 MINUTES | **MAKES:** 4 SERVINGS

INGREDIENTS

2 cans (15 ounces each) pinto beans, rinsed, drained

1 can (15 ounces) diced tomatoes

5 corn tortillas, torn in 3-inch pieces

1 large green bell pepper, chopped

1 large onion, peeled, chopped

1 1/2 tablespoons chili powder

1/2 teaspoon ground cumin

1 teaspoon salt

2 cups grated white cheddar cheese, for serving

DIRECTIONS

1 Place all ingredients, except cheddar cheese, into the pot. Stir to combine, then cover pot.

2 Select Auto-iQ Quick Meals: Recipe 31 and press the START/STOP button.

3 Add cheese. Stir and serve.

SWAPS

Black beans for pinto beans

Corn chips for corn tortillas

RECIPE
32

CHICKPEA CURRY

GF DF VE

PREP: 15 MINUTES | **COOK:** 30 MINUTES | **MAKES:** 4 SERVINGS

INGREDIENTS

1 can (13.66 ounces) unsweetened full-fat coconut milk

1 teaspoon lime juice

2 teaspoons curry powder

1 can (14.5 ounces) diced tomatoes

Salt and pepper, to taste

1/2 teaspoon fresh ginger, grated

1 clove garlic, peeled, minced

1 small onion, peeled, diced (about 1/2 cup)

2 cans (15.5 ounces each) chickpeas, rinsed, drained

1/2 small bunch kale, sliced (about 2 1/2 cups)

Tip: For a complete meal, serve this with naan or pita bread.

DIRECTIONS

1 In a large bowl, whisk together the coconut milk, lime juice, and curry powder until combined. Stir in the tomatoes and their juices, then season with salt and pepper.

2 Transfer mixture to the pot along with remaining ingredients. Stir to combine, then cover pot.

3 **Select Auto-iQ Quick Meals: Recipe 32 and press the START/STOP button.**

4 Stir and serve.

SWAP

Spinach for kale

Meal need to be cooked a little longer? Simply set to BAKE DRY at 350°F for 5-10 minutes, checking for desired doneness.

RECIPE
33

VEGETARIAN TORTILLA SOUP (GF) (DF) (VE)

PREP: 15 MINUTES | **COOK:** 25 MINUTES | **MAKES:** 6 SERVINGS

INGREDIENTS

4 cups low-sodium
vegetable broth

2 cups water

1 can (10.75 ounces)
condensed tomato soup

1 can (15 ounces)
dark red kidney beans

2 cups frozen classic
mixed vegetables

2 cloves garlic,
peeled, minced

1 teaspoon ground cumin

$1/2$ teaspoon
onion powder

$1/2$ teaspoon
dried oregano

$1/4$ teaspoon
smoked paprika

$1/4$ teaspoon ground
black pepper

20 corn tortilla chips

$1/2$ teaspoon salt

OPTIONAL

*$1/4$ cup fresh cilantro,
chopped, for serving*

DIRECTIONS

1 Place all ingredients into the pot. Stir to combine,
then cover pot.

**2 Select Auto-iQ Quick Meals: Recipe 33 and press
the START/STOP button.**

3 Stir and serve.

SWAPS

1 can (15 ounces) crushed tomatoes for condensed
tomato soup

Black beans for kidney beans

ASIAN POT STICKER SOUP

PREP: 10 MINUTES | **COOK:** 25 MINUTES | **MAKES:** 4–5 SERVINGS

INGREDIENTS

2 bags (7 ounces each) frozen pot stickers

1 bag (16 ounces) frozen Asian vegetable blend

3 cups fresh baby spinach

4 cups low-sodium vegetable broth

1/4 cup stir-fry sauce

3 tablespoons low-sodium teriyaki sauce

1/4 teaspoon ground ginger

DIRECTIONS

1 Place all ingredients into the pot. Stir to combine, then cover pot.

2 Select Auto-iQ Quick Meals: Recipe 34 and press the START/STOP button.

3 Serve immediately.

SWAPS

Frozen stir-fry vegetables for Asian vegetable blend

Bok choy for spinach

Chicken broth for vegetable broth

VEGETABLE PAD THAI (DF) (VE) A

PREP: 10 MINUTES | **COOK:** 25 MINUTES | **MAKES:** 4–6 SERVINGS

INGREDIENTS

3/4 package (12 ounces) uncooked linguine, broken in half

3 carrots, peeled, thinly sliced

1 red bell pepper, thinly sliced

4 scallions, trimmed, thinly sliced

4 cloves garlic, peeled, minced

2 teaspoons fresh ginger, minced

3 1/2 cups vegetable broth

1 tablespoon peanut butter

3 tablespoons soy sauce

1 tablespoon brown sugar

1/2 teaspoon crushed red pepper

1 cup fresh cilantro, finely chopped, plus more for serving

Juice of 1 lime

OPTIONAL

1/2 cup chopped peanuts, for serving

Lime wedges, for serving

DIRECTIONS

1 Place all ingredients into the pot. Stir to combine, ensuring pasta is submerged, then cover pot.

2 Select Auto-iQ Quick Meals: Recipe 35 and press the START/STOP button.

3 Stir and serve.

SWAP

1 package whole wheat spaghetti for linguine

Meal need to be cooked a little longer? Simply set to BAKE DRY at 350°F for 5-10 minutes, checking for desired doneness.

RECIPE 36

PINTO BEAN & VEGETABLE ENCHILADA CASSEROLE (GF) (DF) (VG) (VE) (A)

PREP: 5 MINUTES | **COOK:** 25 MINUTES | **MAKES:** 6–8 SERVINGS

INGREDIENTS

2 cans (10 ounces each) mild enchilada sauce

2 cans (4.5 ounces each) chopped green chiles

1 tablespoon ground cumin

1/4 teaspoon ground black pepper

2 bell peppers, sliced

16 soft corn tortillas, cut in quarters

2 cans (15 ounces each) pinto beans, rinsed, drained

OPTIONAL
1 1/2 cups shredded Mexican cheese, for serving

DIRECTIONS

1 In a mixing bowl, stir together enchilada sauce, green chiles, cumin, and black pepper.

2 Place peppers, corn tortillas, pinto beans, and sauce mixture into the pot. Stir to combine, then cover pot.

3 Select Auto-iQ Quick Meals: Recipe 36 and press the START/STOP button.

SWAPS

Red chiles for green chiles

Black beans for pinto beans

RECIPE 37

TOFU LENTIL STEW (GF) (DF) (VE)

PREP: 5 MINUTES | **COOK:** 25 MINUTES | **MAKES:** 4 SERVINGS

INGREDIENTS

1 brick (14 ounces) extra-firm tofu, drained, cut in 1/2-inch chunks

2 2/3 cups vegetable broth

2/3 cup uncooked red lentils

1 can (14.5 ounces) petite diced tomatoes

3 cups bok choy, chopped

1 tablespoon Italian seasoning

1/4 teaspoon ground black pepper

DIRECTIONS

1 Place all ingredients into the pot. Stir to combine, then cover pot.

2 Select Auto-iQ Quick Meals: Recipe 37 and press the START/STOP button.

SWAPS

1 medium zucchini, chopped or 1 pound uncooked chicken breast, cut in 1-inch cubes for tofu

Kale or Chinese cabbage for bok choy

2 tablespoons curry paste for Italian seasoning

Tip: Serve with fresh sprouts, cilantro, and lime wedges.

RECIPE 38

PIEROGI WITH HORSERADISH SAUCE

(VG)

PREP: 10 MINUTES | **COOK:** 25 MINUTES | **MAKES:** 6 SERVINGS

INGREDIENTS

2 pounds frozen pierogi

1 medium onion, peeled, chopped

2 cups vegetable broth

3 cups fresh baby spinach

2 tablespoons prepared horseradish

¼ teaspoon kosher salt

¼ teaspoon ground black pepper

DIRECTIONS

1 Place all ingredients into the pot. Gently stir to combine, then cover pot.

2 Select Auto-iQ Quick Meals: Recipe 38 and press the START/STOP button.

SWAP

Large frozen ravioli for pierogi

> **Tip:** Serve with a side of sour cream or Greek yogurt.

RECIPE 39

CUBAN-STYLE BLACK BEANS (GF) (DF) (VE)

PREP: 5 MINUTES | **COOK:** 20 MINUTES | **MAKES:** 6-8 SERVINGS

INGREDIENTS

3 cans (15.5 ounces each) black beans, rinsed, drained

1 can (15.5 ounces) white hominy, rinsed, drained

1 small white onion, peeled, finely chopped

2 cloves garlic, peeled, minced

2 bay leaves

1 teaspoon ground cumin

1 teaspoon salt

1 ⅓ cup vegetable stock

2 teaspoons dried Mexican oregano

DIRECTIONS

1 Place all ingredients into the pot. Stir to combine, then cover pot.

2 Select Auto-iQ Quick Meals: Recipe 39 and press the START/STOP button.

3 Stir and serve.

> **Tip:** Serve with plenty of fresh toppings like sliced avocado, sliced radishes, chopped cilantro, and Mexican cheese like cotija or queso fresco.

Meal need to be cooked a little longer? Simply set to BAKE DRY at 350°F for 5-10 minutes, checking for desired doneness.

DO A 1-2 STEP TO DELICIOUS

LAYERED BOWLS

These 2-step recipes use your Auto-iQ Cooking System to build some serious flavor. Yep, these layered bowls featuring hearty blends of proteins and veggies will have your taste buds dancing.

BREAKFAST

BEEF

PORK

POULTRY

SEAFOOD

VEGETARIAN

> Meal need to be cooked a little longer?
> Simply set to BAKE DRY at 350°F for 5–10
> minutes, checking for desired doneness.

BAKED EGGS WITH BREAKFAST HASH

GF

PREP: 15 MINUTES | **COOK:** 29 MINUTES | **MAKES:** 4 SERVINGS

INGREDIENTS

2 tablespoons butter

1 pound uncooked ground breakfast sausage, crumbled

1 large Idaho potato, diced

2 bell peppers, diced

1 medium white onion, peeled, diced

1 teaspoon garlic powder

1 teaspoon onion powder

2 teaspoons salt

1 teaspoon ground black pepper

8 eggs

¼ cup maple syrup

OPTIONAL

1 teaspoon paprika, for serving

DIRECTIONS

1 Set to STOVE TOP HIGH and preheat pot for 5 minutes. Heat butter in pot for 2 minutes and add breakfast sausage, potato, bell peppers, onion, garlic powder, onion powder, salt, and pepper. Cook, uncovered, for 15 minutes, stirring occasionally.

2 Crack the eggs on top of the hash. Pour maple syrup evenly over top, then cover pot. **Select Auto-iQ Layered Bowls: Recipe 1 and press the START/STOP button.** Serve immediately.

BUTTERNUT HASH & EGGS

GF

PREP: 20 MINUTES | **COOK:** 30 MINUTES | **MAKES:** 4 SERVINGS

INGREDIENTS

1 teaspoon butter

1 package (4 ounces) diced pancetta

1 butternut squash, peeled, cut in 1-inch pieces

1 medium shallot, peeled, chopped

1 jalapeño pepper, diced

1 sprig fresh thyme leaves

4 eggs

OPTIONAL

1 teaspoon fresh parsley, chopped, for garnish

DIRECTIONS

1 Set to STOVE TOP HIGH and preheat pot for 5 minutes. Heat butter in pot for 2 minutes and add pancetta, squash, shallot, jalapeño pepper, and thyme. Cook for 15 minutes, stirring occasionally.

2 Crack eggs on top of squash mixture. **Select Auto-iQ Layered Bowls: Recipe 2 and press the START/STOP button.** Stir and serve.

SWAP

Bacon for pancetta

Tip: For a spicier dish, look for a red jalapeño pepper instead of a green one.

**RECIPE
3**

BEEF FAJITA RICE BOWL (GF) (DF)

PREP: 15 MINUTES | **COOK:** 47 MINUTES | **MAKES:** 4-6 SERVINGS

INGREDIENTS

1 tablespoon canola oil

1 1/2 pounds uncooked beef flank steak, cut in 2-inch x 1/4-inch slices

2 packets (1.25 ounces each) fajita seasoning mix

2 bell peppers, thinly sliced

1 medium onion, peeled, thinly sliced

2 1/2 cups low-sodium beef broth

1 cup uncooked long grain white rice

OPTIONAL
Guacamole, for serving

Salsa, for serving

Sour cream, for serving

DIRECTIONS

1 Set to STOVE TOP HIGH and preheat pot for 5 minutes. Heat oil in pot for 2 minutes and then add flank steak, fajita seasoning mix, bell peppers, and onion. Cook uncovered for 10 minutes, stirring occasionally.

2 Add broth and rice to pot. Stir to combine, then cover pot. **Select Auto-iQ Layered Bowls: Recipe 3 and press the START/STOP button.** Stir and serve.

Tip: To turn this bowl into a burrito—just warm large soft flour tortillas and wrap up the finished product.

Meal need to be cooked a little longer? Simply set to BAKE DRY at 350°F for 5-10 minutes, checking for desired doneness.

RECIPE 4

AMERICAN CHOP SUEY

PREP: 10 MINUTES | **COOK:** 35 MINUTES | **MAKES:** 6 SERVINGS

INGREDIENTS

1 tablespoon canola oil

1 pound uncooked ground beef

1 red bell pepper, chopped

1 medium onion, peeled, chopped

1 box (16 ounces) uncooked elbow macaroni

1 jar (24 ounces) pasta sauce

4 cups water

¼ cup Worcestershire sauce

½ teaspoon ground black pepper

¼ teaspoon kosher salt

OPTIONAL
2 cups shredded mozzarella cheese, for serving

DIRECTIONS

1 Set to STOVE TOP HIGH and preheat pot for 5 minutes. Heat oil in pot for 2 minutes and then add ground beef, red bell pepper, and onion. Cook uncovered for 8 minutes, stirring occasionally.

2 Add macaroni, pasta sauce, water, Worcestershire sauce, black pepper, and salt to pot. Stir to combine, then cover pot. **Select Auto-iQ Layered Bowls: Recipe 4 and press the START/STOP button.** Stir and serve.

SWAPS

Ground turkey for ground beef

Ditalini pasta for elbow macaroni

RECIPE 5

SWEET & SPICY BEEF WITH EDAMAME

PREP: 15 MINUTES | **COOK:** 42 MINUTES | **MAKES:** 4-6 SERVINGS

INGREDIENTS

1 tablespoon canola oil

1 1/2 pounds uncooked beef flank steak, cut in 2-inch by 1/4-inch slices

1 red bell pepper, thinly sliced

1 medium carrot, peeled, thinly sliced

1 tablespoon fresh ginger, minced

1 1/2 cups low-sodium beef broth

1 cup uncooked jasmine rice

1 cup frozen shelled edamame

1/3 cup sweet chili sauce

1 tablespoon sambal oelek (or any red chili sauce or paste)

OPTIONAL
1 can (11 ounces) mandarin oranges, drained, for serving

DIRECTIONS

1 Set to STOVE TOP HIGH and preheat pot for 5 minutes. Heat oil in pot for 2 minutes and then add flank steak, red bell pepper, carrot, and ginger. Cook uncovered for 10 minutes, stirring occasionally.

2 Add broth, rice, edamame, chili sauce, and sambal oelek to pot. Stir to combine, then cover pot. **Select Auto-iQ Layered Bowls: Recipe 5 and press the START/STOP button.** Stir and serve.

RECIPE 6

BEEF BARLEY STROGANOFF

PREP: 15 MINUTES | **COOK:** 42 MINUTES | **MAKES:** 8 SERVINGS

INGREDIENTS

1 tablespoon canola oil

1 1/2 pounds uncooked lean ground beef

2 medium carrots, peeled, chopped

1 medium onion, peeled, chopped

3 cloves garlic, peeled, minced

1 can or jar (10.5 ounces) beef gravy

3 cups low-sodium beef broth

1 pound white mushrooms, chopped

1/2 cup uncooked barley

2 tablespoons Worcestershire sauce

1 tablespoon Dijon mustard

1 teaspoon paprika

1/4 teaspoon ground black pepper

OPTIONAL
1/2 cup sour cream, for serving

DIRECTIONS

1 Set to STOVE TOP HIGH and preheat pot for 5 minutes. Heat oil in pot for 2 minutes and then add beef, carrots, onion, and garlic. Cook uncovered for 10 minutes, stirring occasionally.

2 Add gravy, broth, mushrooms, barley, Worcestershire sauce, mustard, paprika, and black pepper to pot. Stir to combine, then cover pot. **Select Auto-iQ Layered Bowls: Recipe 6 and press the START/STOP button.** Stir and serve.

SWAPS

Ground turkey for ground beef

Greek yogurt for sour cream

Meal need to be cooked a little longer? Simply set to BAKE DRY at 350°F for 5-10 minutes, checking for desired doneness.

RECIPE 7

CHEESEBURGER PASTA

PREP: 15 MINUTES | **COOK:** 38 MINUTES | **MAKES:** 6 SERVINGS

INGREDIENTS

1 ½ pounds uncooked ground beef

1 medium white onion, peeled, diced

1 tablespoon kosher salt

1 can (14 ounces) crushed tomatoes

½ cup ketchup

½ cup yellow mustard

½ cup relish

¾ box (12 ounces) uncooked large pasta shells

3 cups water

1 cup shredded cheddar cheese

OPTIONAL
2 scallions, sliced, for garnish

DIRECTIONS

1 Set to STOVE TOP HIGH and preheat pot for 5 minutes. Add beef, onion, and salt and cook, stirring occasionally, for 5 minutes.

2 Add tomatoes, ketchup, mustard, relish, pasta, and water to pot. Gently stir to combine and cover pot. **Select Auto-iQ Layered Bowls: Recipe 7 and press the START/STOP button.** Stir in cheese and serve.

SWAPS

Ground chicken for ground beef

Penne pasta for shells

RECIPE 8

FREEFORM BEEF & ARTICHOKE LASAGNA

PREP: 20 MINUTES | **COOK:** 37 MINUTES | **MAKES:** 6 SERVINGS

INGREDIENTS

2 tablespoons canola oil

1 ½ pounds uncooked ground beef

3 cloves garlic, peeled, minced

1 medium white onion, peeled, chopped

2 tablespoons kosher salt

1 box (9 ounces) uncooked oven-ready lasagna noodles, broken in 2-inch pieces

1 jar (8 ounces) cooked artichoke hearts, drained, cut in half

1 cup (8 ounces) ricotta cheese

1 jar (24 ounces) prepared pasta sauce

OPTIONAL
1 bag (5 ounces) baby spinach, for serving

1 cup shredded mozzarella cheese, for serving

DIRECTIONS

1 Set to STOVE TOP HIGH and preheat pot for 5 minutes. Heat oil in pot for 2 minutes and then add beef, garlic, onion, and salt. Cook for 10 minutes, stirring occasionally.

2 Add lasagna noodles, artichoke hearts, ricotta, and pasta sauce to the pot. Stir to combine, then cover pot. **Select Auto-iQ Layered Bowls: Recipe 8 and press the START/STOP button.** Stir and serve.

SWAPS

Ground chicken for ground beef

Sundried tomatoes for artichoke hearts

TORTELLINI WITH SAUSAGE ALFREDO

PREP: 15 MINUTES | **COOK:** 30 MINUTES | **MAKES:** 4-6 SERVINGS

INGREDIENTS

1 tablespoon olive oil

2 cloves garlic, peeled, minced

1 small white onion, peeled, chopped

1 pound uncooked spicy Italian sausage, sliced in 1-inch pieces

1 jar (15 ounces) Alfredo sauce

1 cup water

2 pounds frozen cheese tortellini

OPTIONAL

$1/2$ cup grated Parmesan cheese, for serving

DIRECTIONS

1 Set to STOVE TOP HIGH and preheat pot for 5 minutes. Heat oil in pot for 2 minutes and then add garlic, onion, and sausage. Sauté 4 minutes, or until sausage is browned, stirring occasionally.

2 Add Alfredo sauce, water, and tortellini to pot. Stir to combine, then cover pot. **Select Auto-iQ Layered Bowls: Recipe 9 and press the START/STOP button.** Stir and serve.

PORK CHOPS WITH APPLES & RICE

(GF) (DF)

PREP: 15 MINUTES | **COOK:** 47 MINUTES | **MAKES:** 4 SERVINGS

INGREDIENTS

1 tablespoon canola oil

4 uncooked boneless pork chops, 1-inch thick

2 cups shredded red cabbage

$1/2$ medium onion, peeled, chopped

$2 1/2$ cups low-sodium chicken broth

1 cup uncooked long grain white rice

2 tablespoons apple cider vinegar

1 tablespoon whole grain mustard

$3/4$ teaspoon kosher salt

$1/2$ teaspoon ground black pepper

$1/4$ teaspoon ground sage

2 apples, cored, cut in quarters

DIRECTIONS

1 Set to STOVE TOP HIGH and preheat pot for 5 minutes. Heat oil in pot for 2 minutes and then add pork chops, cabbage, and onion. Cook uncovered for 10 minutes, stirring occasionally.

2 Add remaining ingredients to pot. Stir to combine, then cover pot. **Select Auto-iQ Layered Bowls: Recipe 10 and press the START/STOP button.** Serve immediately.

SWAPS

Turkey cutlets for pork chops

Pears for apples

Meal need to be cooked a little longer? Simply set to BAKE DRY at 350°F for 5-10 minutes, checking for desired doneness.

SAUSAGE WITH BUTTER BEANS

SAUSAGE WITH BUTTER BEANS (GF) (DF)

PREP: 15 MINUTES | **COOK:** 25 MINUTES | **MAKES:** 4 SERVINGS

INGREDIENTS

1 tablespoon extra virgin olive oil

1 package (16 ounces) smoked andouille sausage, sliced

2 cans (15 ounces each) butter beans, rinsed, drained

3/4 cup chicken stock

3 shallots, peeled, finely chopped

2 cloves garlic, peeled, finely chopped

2–3 sprigs fresh thyme, leaves roughly chopped

DIRECTIONS

1 Set to STOVE TOP HIGH and preheat pot for 5 minutes. Heat oil in pot for 2 minutes and then add sausage. Cook, stirring occasionally, until browned on both sides, about 8 minutes.

2 Add beans, stock, shallots, garlic, and thyme to the pot. Stir to combine, then cover pot. **Select Auto-iQ Layered Bowls: Recipe 11 and press the START/STOP button.**

SWAPS

Smoked chorizo for andouille sausage

Cannellini beans for butter beans

Tip: To lighten up this dish, add 3 cups baby spinach, chopped mustard greens, or chopped kale when adding the stock.

ORECCHIETTE WITH BROCCOLI RABE & SAUSAGE (DF)

PREP: 15 MINUTES | **COOK:** 34 MINUTES | **MAKES:** 6 SERVINGS

INGREDIENTS

2 tablespoons extra virgin olive oil

1 pound uncooked sweet Italiansausage, casings removed

1 small yellow onion, peeled, finely chopped

4 medium cloves garlic, peeled, minced

1 teaspoon salt

1/4 teaspoon ground black pepper

1 bunch broccoli rabe, cut in 2-inch pieces, tough stems removed

1/4 teaspoon crushed red pepper

4 cups chicken broth

6 sundried tomatoes packed in oil, thinly sliced (about 1/2 cup)

1/2 pound uncooked orecchiette pasta (about 2 1/2 cups)

1 teaspoon lemon zest

DIRECTIONS

1 Set to STOVE TOP HIGH and preheat pot for 5 minutes. Heat oil in pot for 2 minutes and then add sausage, onion, and garlic. Cook uncovered, breaking sausage apart, for about 10 minutes, or until sausage is no longer pink.

2 Add the salt, pepper, broccoli rabe, crushed red pepper, broth, sundried tomatoes, orecchiette, and lemon zest to pot. Gently stir to combine, then cover pot. **Select Auto-iQ Layered Bowls: Recipe 12 and press the START/STOP button.** Stir and serve.

Meal need to be cooked a little longer? Simply set to BAKE DRY at 350°F for 5-10 minutes, checking for desired doneness.

SAUSAGE & PEPPERS RICE BOWL

RECIPE 13

PREP: 20 MINUTES | **COOK:** 42 MINUTES | **MAKES:** 4-6 SERVINGS

INGREDIENTS

2 tablespoons olive oil

2 medium onions, peeled, chopped

2 bell peppers, chopped

4 cloves garlic, peeled, minced

1 package (16 ounces) smoked sausage, sliced

1 1/2 cups uncooked jasmine rice

3 cups chicken broth

1 1/2 teaspoons salt

1 teaspoon dried oregano

1/2 teaspoon garlic powder

1/2 teaspoon dried basil

1/4 teaspoon crushed red pepper

DIRECTIONS

1 Set to STOVE TOP HIGH and preheat pot for 5 minutes. Heat oil in pot for 2 minutes and then add onions, bell peppers, and garlic. Cook uncovered for 10 minutes, stirring occasionally.

2 Add all remaining ingredients to pot. Stir to combine, then cover pot. **Select Auto-iQ Layered Bowls: Recipe 13 and press the START/STOP button.** Stir and serve.

SWAPS

Kielbasa for smoked sausage

Basmati rice for jasmine rice

HAM WITH PINEAPPLE RICE

RECIPE 14

(GF) (DF)

PREP: 15 MINUTES | **COOK:** 47 MINUTES | **MAKES:** 4-6 SERVINGS

INGREDIENTS

1 tablespoon canola oil

1 1/2 pounds cooked ham steaks, cut in 1/2-inch pieces

2 medium carrots, peeled, chopped

1 medium onion, peeled, chopped

1 1/2 cups low-sodium chicken broth

1 cup pineapple juice

1 cup uncooked long grain white rice

1/2 cup unsalted dry-roasted whole cashews

1/2 teaspoon kosher salt

1/4 teaspoon ground black pepper

OPTIONAL

1 cup pineapple, chopped, for serving

1/4 cup scallions, chopped, for serving

DIRECTIONS

1 Set to STOVE TOP HIGH and preheat pot for 5 minutes. Heat oil in pot for 2 minutes and then add ham, carrots, and onion. Cook uncovered for 10 minutes, stirring occasionally.

2 Add broth, pineapple juice, rice, cashews, salt, and black pepper to pot. Stir to combine, then cover pot. **Select Auto-iQ Layered Bowls: Recipe 14 and press the START/STOP button.** Stir and serve.

SWAPS

Cooked chicken sausage for ham steak

Jasmine or basmati rice for long grain white rice

RECIPE 15

JAMBALAYA

PREP: 20 MINUTES | **COOK:** 42 MINUTES | **MAKES:** 6 SERVINGS

(GF) (DF)

INGREDIENTS

1 1/2 pounds uncooked boneless, skinless chicken breasts, cut in 1-inch cubes

2 tablespoons Cajun spice, divided

2 tablespoons salt, divided

1 tablespoon ground black pepper, divided

2 tablespoons canola oil

1 pound cooked andouille sausage, chopped

1 medium onion, peeled, chopped

2 green bell peppers, chopped

5 cloves garlic, peeled, chopped

1 1/2 cups chicken stock

1 can (28 ounces) diced fire-roasted tomatoes

2 cups uncooked jasmine rice

DIRECTIONS

1 Season chicken with 1 tablespoon Cajun spice, 1 tablespoon salt, and 1/2 tablespoon black pepper. Set to STOVE TOP HIGH and preheat pot for 5 minutes. Heat oil in pot for 2 minutes, then add chicken, sausage, onion, peppers, and garlic. Cook, uncovered, for 15 minutes, stirring occasionally.

2 Add the chicken stock, tomatoes, rice, and remaining Cajun spice, salt, and pepper to pot. Stir gently to combine, then cover pot. **Select Auto-iQ Layered Bowls: Recipe 15 and press the START/STOP button.** Serve immediately.

RECIPE 16

MUSHROOM PORK CHOPS

PREP: 15 MINUTES | **COOK:** 40 MINUTES | **MAKES:** 4 SERVINGS

INGREDIENTS

4 uncooked boneless pork chops (6 ounces each)

2 tablespoons kosher salt

2 teaspoons ground black pepper

2 tablespoons canola oil

1 can (10 ounces) condensed cream of mushroom soup

1 pint (6 ounces) button mushrooms, cut in quarters

1 white onion, peeled, diced

3/4 box (12 ounces) uncooked bowtie pasta

3 cups water

OPTIONAL
2 tablespoons fresh parsley, minced, for garnish

DIRECTIONS

1 Season pork chops with salt and pepper. Set to STOVE TOP HIGH and preheat pot for 5 minutes. Heat oil in pot for 2 minutes and then add seasoned pork chops. Sear for 5 minutes on each side. Remove pork from pot and set aside.

2 Add mushroom soup, mushrooms, onion, pasta, and water to the pot. Stir to combine. Place pork chops on top of mushroom mixture, then cover pot. **Select Auto-iQ Layered Bowls: Recipe 16 and press the START/STOP button.**

SWAP

Chicken breast for pork chops

Meal need to be cooked a little longer? Simply set to BAKE DRY at 350°F for 5–10 minutes, checking for desired doneness.

PEANUT CHICKEN WITH CAULIFLOWER RICE

PEANUT CHICKEN WITH CAULIFLOWER RICE

(DF)

PREP: 30 MINUTES | **COOK:** 25 MINUTES | **MAKES:** 4 SERVINGS

INGREDIENTS

2 teaspoons canola oil

1 1/2 pounds uncooked boneless, skinless chicken breasts, cut in cubes

1/2 cup low-sodium soy sauce

3 tablespoons peanut butter

1–2 teaspoons sriracha (optional)

1 bunch scallions, roughly chopped

4 cups (12 ounces) cauliflower florets, finely chopped (about 1 head cauliflower)

1 bag (8 ounces) snap peas, trimmed

OPTIONAL
Peanuts, chopped, for serving

DIRECTIONS

1 Set to STOVE TOP HIGH and preheat pot for 5 minutes. Heat oil in pot for 2 minutes and then add chicken. Cook, stirring occasionally, until chicken is golden brown and mostly cooked through, about 10 minutes.

2 Add soy sauce, peanut butter, and sriracha to the pot. Stir to combine. Layer scallions, cauliflower, and peas on top of chicken mixture. Cover pot. **Select Auto-iQ Layered Bowls: Recipe 17 and press the START/STOP button.** Stir and serve.

CHICKEN PHO

(GF) (DF) A

PREP: 20 MINUTES | **COOK:** 32 MINUTES | **MAKES:** 6 SERVINGS

INGREDIENTS

2 tablespoons canola oil

3 uncooked boneless, skinless chicken breasts (about 1 1/4 pounds), cut in 1-inch cubes

4 cloves garlic, peeled, chopped

2 tablespoons lemongrass, minced

1 tablespoon fresh ginger, chopped

2 cartons (32 ounces each) chicken stock

4 cups bok choy, cleaned

1 tablespoon fish sauce

1 sleeve (6 ounces) uncooked cellophane rice noodles

OPTIONAL
8 scallions, sliced, for serving

DIRECTIONS

1 Set to STOVE TOP HIGH and preheat pot for 5 minutes. Heat oil in pot for 2 minutes and then add chicken, garlic, lemongrass, and ginger. Cook for 10 minutes, stirring occasionally.

2 Add the chicken stock, bok choy, fish sauce, and rice noodles to pot. Stir to combine, then cover pot. **Select Auto-iQ Layered Bowls: Recipe 18 and press the START/STOP button.** Stir and serve.

SWAP

Large shrimp, peeled, deveined, for chicken breasts

Meal need to be cooked a little longer? Simply set to BAKE DRY at 350°F for 5-10 minutes, checking for desired doneness.

Questions? 1-877-646-5288 | ninjakitchen.com   71

RECIPE 19

MEDITERRANEAN CHICKEN TENDERS

(DF) (A)

PREP: 10 MINUTES | **COOK:** 31 MINUTES | **MAKES:** 4 SERVINGS

INGREDIENTS

2 tablespoons olive oil

1 pound uncooked chicken tenderloins

1 medium onion, peeled, chopped

3 cloves garlic, peeled, minced

1 teaspoon lemon pepper seasoning

$^3/_4$ teaspoon dried oregano

2 $^2/_3$ cups low-sodium chicken broth

1 cup uncooked orzo

1 cup frozen peas

$^1/_2$ cup sundried tomatoes, chopped

$^1/_3$ cup sliced black olives

DIRECTIONS

1 Set to STOVE TOP HIGH and preheat pot for 5 minutes. Heat oil in pot for 2 minutes and then add chicken, onion, garlic, lemon pepper seasoning, and oregano. Cook uncovered for 7 minutes, stirring occasionally.

2 Add remaining ingredients to pot. Stir to combine, then cover pot. **Select Auto-iQ Layered Bowls: Recipe 19 and press the START/STOP button.** Serve immediately.

RECIPE 20

ARROZ CON POLLO

(GF) (DF)

PREP: 20 MINUTES | **COOK:** 47 MINUTES | **MAKES:** 6 SERVINGS

INGREDIENTS

1 tablespoon canola oil

1 $^1/_2$ pounds uncooked boneless skinless chicken thighs

1 medium onion, peeled, chopped

3 cloves garlic, peeled, minced

2 $^3/_4$ cups low-sodium chicken broth

1 cup uncooked long grain white rice

1 cup frozen peas

1 teaspoon dried oregano

1 tablespoon ground cumin

$^1/_4$ teaspoon kosher salt

OPTIONAL

$^1/_3$ cup fresh cilantro, chopped, for serving

DIRECTIONS

1 Set to STOVE TOP HIGH and preheat pot for 5 minutes. Heat oil in pot for 2 minutes and then add chicken, onion, and garlic. Cook uncovered for 10 minutes, stirring occasionally.

2 Add broth, rice, peas, oregano, cumin, and salt to pot. Stir to combine, then cover pot. **Select Auto-iQ Layered Bowls: Recipe 20 and press the START/STOP button.** Stir and serve.

SWAPS

Chicken breasts for chicken thighs

Yellow rice for long grain white rice

**RECIPE
21**

CREAMY FRENCH ONION CHICKEN & RICE

PREP: 15 MINUTES | **COOK:** 52 MINUTES | **MAKES:** 4-5 SERVINGS

INGREDIENTS

1 ¹/₂ tablespoons canola oil

1 medium onion, peeled, chopped

1 carrot, peeled, chopped

¹/₂ cup celery, chopped

1 packet (1.4 ounces) dry French onion soup mix

1 can (10.5 ounces) condensed cream of chicken soup

1 rotisserie chicken, shredded (about 4 cups shredded chicken)

3 cups water

1 cup uncooked long grain white rice

OPTIONAL
1 ¹/₂ cups shredded mild cheddar cheese, for serving

DIRECTIONS

1 Set to STOVE TOP HIGH and preheat pot for 5 minutes. Heat oil in pot for 2 minutes and then add onion, carrot, and celery. Cook uncovered for 5 minutes, stirring occasionally.

2 Add French onion soup mix, cream of chicken soup, chicken, water, and rice to pot. Stir to combine, then cover pot. **Select Auto-iQ Layered Bowls: Recipe 21 and press the START/STOP button.** Stir and serve.

Meal need to be cooked a little longer? Simply set to BAKE DRY at 350°F for 5-10 minutes, checking for desired doneness.

RECIPE
22

SOUTHWEST CHICKEN BURRITO BOWL

(GF) (DF)

PREP: 15 MINUTES | **COOK:** 42 MINUTES | **MAKES:** 6 SERVINGS

INGREDIENTS

2 teaspoons chili powder

$1/2$ teaspoon
ground cumin

$1/4$ teaspoon
garlic powder

$1/2$ teaspoon kosher salt

1 pound uncooked
chicken tenderloins,
cut in half lengthwise

2 teaspoons olive oil

1 small onion,
peeled, chopped

$3/4$ cup red or yellow bell
pepper, diced

1 can (15 ounces) black
beans, rinsed, drained

2 $1/2$ cups chicken broth

1 box (7 ounces) yellow
Spanish rice

OPTIONAL

$1/4$ cup fresh cilantro,
chopped, for serving

Sour cream, for serving

Shredded cheddar
cheese, for serving

DIRECTIONS

1 In a small bowl, stir together the chili powder,
cumin, garlic powder, and salt. Season the chicken
with half the spice mixture. Set to STOVE TOP HIGH
and preheat pot for 5 minutes. Heat oil in pot for
2 minutes and then add seasoned chicken, onion,
and bell pepper. Sauté until chicken is lightly
browned, about 5 minutes.

2 Add remaining spice mixture, beans, broth,
and rice to pot. Stir to combine, then cover pot.
**Select Auto-iQ Layered Bowls: Recipe 22 and press
the START/STOP button.** Stir and serve.

RECIPE 23

CHICKEN GYRO WITH QUINOA (GF) (DF) (A)

PREP: 15 MINUTES | **COOK:** 40 MINUTES | **MAKES:** 6 SERVINGS

INGREDIENTS

1 tablespoon canola oil

2 pounds uncooked boneless, skinless chicken thighs, cut in 1-inch pieces

1 green bell pepper, chopped

1 onion, peeled, sliced

2 ¾ cups low-sodium chicken broth

1 cup uncooked quinoa

4 cloves garlic, peeled, minced

1 1/2 teaspoons dried oregano

1/2 teaspoon kosher salt

1/2 teaspoon ground black pepper

OPTIONAL

1 1/2 cups cherry tomatoes, cut in half, for serving

1 cup crumbled feta cheese, for serving

1 cup tzatziki sauce, for serving

DIRECTIONS

1 Set to STOVE TOP HIGH and preheat pot for 5 minutes. Heat oil in pot for 2 minutes and then add chicken thighs, bell pepper, and onion. Cook uncovered for 10 minutes, stirring occasionally.

2 Add broth, quinoa, garlic, oregano, salt, and black pepper to pot. Stir to combine, then cover pot. **Select Auto-iQ Layered Bowls: Recipe 23 and press the START/STOP button.** Stir and serve.

SWAPS

Chicken breasts for chicken thighs

Basmati rice for quinoa

RECIPE 24

CHICKEN WITH MUSHROOM MARSALA COUSCOUS (A)

PREP: 15 MINUTES | **COOK:** 32 MINUTES | **MAKES:** 4 SERVINGS

INGREDIENTS

2 tablespoons butter

3 tablespoons all-purpose flour

1 pound uncooked boneless, skinless chicken breasts, cut in 1 1/2-inch pieces

1 medium onion, peeled, chopped

4 cloves garlic, peeled, minced

2 teaspoons fresh thyme, minced

3/4 teaspoon ground black pepper

2 cups chicken broth

1/3 cup Marsala wine

1 cup uncooked Israeli couscous

1 package (16 ounces) sliced white mushrooms

OPTIONAL

1/4 cup fresh parsley, chopped, for garnish

DIRECTIONS

1 Set to STOVE TOP HIGH and preheat pot for 5 minutes. Heat butter in pot for 2 minutes and add flour, chicken, onion, garlic, thyme, and black pepper. Cook uncovered for 5 minutes, stirring occasionally.

2 Add broth, Marsala, couscous, and mushrooms to pot. Stir to combine, then cover pot. **Select Auto-iQ Layered Bowls: Recipe 24 and press the START/STOP button.** Stir and serve.

SWAP

Cremini mushrooms for sliced white mushrooms

Meal need to be cooked a little longer? Simply set to BAKE DRY at 350°F for 5-10 minutes, checking for desired doneness.

RECIPE 25
CHICKEN WITH MUSTARD CREAM SAUCE

PREP: 10 MINUTES | **COOK:** 37 MINUTES | **MAKES:** 6 SERVINGS

INGREDIENTS

6 uncooked boneless, skinless chicken thighs

1 tablespoon kosher salt

2 tablespoons canola oil

2 1/2 cups chicken stock

1 1/2 cups uncooked jasmine rice

1 cup heavy cream

1/2 cup Dijon mustard

1 tablespoon fresh tarragon, minced

OPTIONAL
2 scallions, sliced, for serving

DIRECTIONS

1 Season chicken with salt. Set to STOVE TOP HIGH and preheat pot for 5 minutes. Heat oil in pot for 2 minutes and then add seasoned chicken. Brown for 5 minutes on each side.

2 Add stock, rice, cream, mustard, and tarragon to pot. Gently stir to combine, then cover pot. **Select Auto-iQ Layered Bowls: Recipe 25 and press the START/STOP button.** Stir and serve.

SWAP

Pork tenderloins for chicken thighs

RECIPE 26
RED WINE CHICKEN (COQ AU VIN)

PREP: 20 MINUTES | **COOK:** 45 MINUTES | **MAKES:** 4 SERVINGS

INGREDIENTS

4 uncooked boneless, skinless chicken thighs

1 tablespoon flour

1 tablespoon butter

3 slices (about 3 ounces) bacon, diced

6 button mushrooms, cut in quarters

1 carrot, peeled, diced

1/2 medium onion, peeled, chopped

2 cups cauliflower florets, finely chopped

1 cup dry red wine

1 1/2 cups chicken stock

DIRECTIONS

1 Coat the chicken thighs in flour. Set to STOVE TOP HIGH and preheat pot for 5 minutes. Add butter, bacon, and chicken to the pot and cook for 10 minutes or until the chicken is golden brown.

2 Flip chicken thighs. Add mushrooms, carrot, onion, cauliflower, red wine, and stock to the pot. **Select Auto-iQ Layered Bowls: Recipe 26 and press the START/STOP button.**

SWAPS

1 package (4 ounces) diced pancetta for bacon

Broccoli rice for cauliflower rice

QUICK CHICKEN CASSOULET (DF)

PREP: 25 MINUTES | **COOK:** 50 MINUTES | **MAKES:** 6 SERVINGS

INGREDIENTS

4 uncooked boneless, skinless chicken thighs, cut in 1-inch pieces

1 package (12 ounces) prepared chicken sausages, sliced

1 package (4 ounces) diced pancetta

2 medium carrots, peeled, diced

1 medium white onion, peeled, diced

3 cloves garlic, peeled, minced

1 tablespoon tomato paste

2 cups chicken stock

2 cans (15 ounces each) cannellini beans, rinsed, drained

1 tablespoon kosher salt

OPTIONAL

5 fresh thyme sprigs, leaves reserved, for garnish

DIRECTIONS

1 Set to STOVE TOP HIGH and preheat pot for 5 minutes. Add chicken, sausages, pancetta, carrots, onion, and garlic to the pot and cook for 10 minutes, stirring occasionally.

2 Add tomato paste, stock, cannellini beans, and salt to the pot. Gently stir to combine, then cover pot. **Select Auto-iQ Layered Bowls: Recipe 27 and press the START/STOP button.** Stir and serve.

SWAP

3 slices cooked bacon, chopped, for pancetta

Meal need to be cooked a little longer? Simply set to BAKE DRY at 350°F for 5–10 minutes, checking for desired doneness.

RECIPE 28

TURKEY & MUSHROOM KASHA

PREP: 15 MINUTES | **COOK:** 35 MINUTES | **MAKES:** 4 SERVINGS

INGREDIENTS

2 tablespoons unsalted butter

1 pound uncooked ground turkey

1 onion, peeled, finely chopped

1 package (12 ounces) button mushrooms, trimmed, cut in half

2 sprigs fresh thyme, leaves roughly chopped

1 cup uncooked medium-ground kasha

2 cups chicken stock

$1/2$ teaspoon salt

DIRECTIONS

1 Set to STOVE TOP HIGH and preheat pot for 5 minutes. Heat butter in pot for 2 minutes and add turkey, onion, and mushrooms. Cook, stirring occasionally, until turkey is crumbled and cooked through and mushrooms are softened, about 15 minutes.

2 Add thyme, kasha, stock, and salt to the pot. Stir to combine. **Select Auto-iQ Layered Bowls: Recipe 28 and press the START/STOP button.**

SWAPS

Ground chicken for ground turkey

Orzo for kasha

Tip: Garnish with finely chopped parsley or chives for a pop of green.

TURKEY MINESTRONE SOUP

(DF)

PREP: 15 MINUTES | **COOK:** 47 MINUTES | **MAKES:** 4 SERVINGS

INGREDIENTS

2 teaspoons extra virgin olive oil

1 pound uncooked lean ground turkey

1 onion, peeled, finely chopped

3 cloves garlic, peeled, finely chopped

3 stalks celery, chopped

4 carrots, peeled, chopped

1/2 head green cabbage, chopped

1 can (15 ounces) diced tomatoes

1 cup water

1/2 box (8 ounces) uncooked ditalini pasta

6 cups chicken stock

Salt and pepper, to taste

Tip: For a heartier soup, add a can of kidney or cannellini beans, drained and rinsed, at Step 2.

DIRECTIONS

1 Set to STOVE TOP HIGH and preheat pot for 5 minutes. Heat oil in pot for 2 minutes and then add turkey, onion, garlic, celery, and carrots. Cook, stirring occasionally, until turkey is crumbled and cooked through and vegetables are beginning to soften, about 15 minutes.

2 Add cabbage, tomatoes, water, pasta, stock, salt, and pepper to the pot. Stir to combine, then cover pot. **Select Auto-iQ Layered Bowls: Recipe 29 and press the START/STOP button.**

SWAPS

Ground chicken for ground turkey

Elbow macaroni pasta for ditalini pasta

Meal need to be cooked a little longer? Simply set to BAKE DRY at 350°F for 5-10 minutes, checking for desired doneness.

SHRIMP & BOK CHOY WITH RICE

SHRIMP & BOK CHOY WITH RICE (DF)

PREP: 20 MINUTES | **COOK:** 32 **MINUTES** | **MAKES:** 4–6 SERVINGS

INGREDIENTS

2 teaspoons canola oil

4 cloves garlic, peeled, minced

2-inch piece fresh ginger, peeled, minced

6 heads baby bok choy, roughly chopped, leafy greens separated

1 cup uncooked long grain white rice

1 1/3 cup water

1/3 cup soy sauce

1 1/2 pounds uncooked shrimp, peeled, deveined

DIRECTIONS

1 Set to STOVE TOP HIGH and preheat pot for 5 minutes. Heat oil in pot for 2 minutes and then add garlic, ginger, and thick ends of bok choy. Sauté until softened, about 5 minutes.

2 Add rice, water, and soy sauce to the pot. Stir to combine. Place shrimp on top of rice mixture, then layer the leafy bok choy greens over the shrimp. Cover pot. **Select Auto-iQ Layered Bowls: Recipe 30 and press the START/STOP button.**

Tip: Serve with extra soy sauce and chopped scallions on the side.

COD WITH BROCCOLI RABE & QUINOA (GF) (DF)

PREP: 15 MINUTES | **COOK:** 27 MINUTES | **MAKES:** 2 SERVINGS

INGREDIENTS

2 tablespoons olive oil

1/2 red bell pepper, chopped

1/2 medium onion, peeled, chopped

2 cloves garlic, peeled, minced

1 2/3 cups low sodium vegetable broth

1/2 cup uncooked quinoa

1/4 teaspoon kosher salt, plus more to taste

1/4 teaspoon ground black pepper, plus more to taste

2 uncooked fresh cod fillets (6 ounces each)

1/2 bunch broccoli rabe, coarse stems trimmed

DIRECTIONS

1 Set to STOVE TOP HIGH and preheat pot for 5 minutes. Heat oil in pot for 2 minutes and then add red bell pepper, onion, garlic, broth, quinoa, salt, and pepper. Cook uncovered for 10 minutes, stirring occasionally.

2 Season cod with additional salt and black pepper. Place cod and broccoli rabe on rack and place rack in pot. Cover pot. **Select Auto-iQ Layered Bowls: Recipe 31 and press the START/STOP button.** Serve immediately.

SWAP

Asparagus for broccoli rabe

Meal need to be cooked a little longer? Simply set to BAKE DRY at 350°F for 5–10 minutes, checking for desired doneness.

NEW ENGLAND CLAM CHOWDER

PREP: 30 MINUTES | **COOK:** 35 MINUTES | **MAKES:** 4 SERVINGS

INGREDIENTS

1 tablespoon butter

3 slices (about 3 ounces) uncooked bacon, diced

2 carrots, peeled, diced

1/2 onion, peeled, chopped

1 pound Yukon gold potatoes, peeled, diced

1 1/2 tablespoons flour

4 cups half & half

1 bottle (8 ounces) clam juice

3 cans (6.5 ounces each) minced clams, drained

1 tablespoon seafood or crab seasoning

OPTIONAL
Oyster crackers, for serving

DIRECTIONS

1 Set to STOVE TOP HIGH and preheat pot for 5 minutes. Add butter, bacon, carrots, onion, and potatoes to the pot and cook for 10 minutes, stirring occasionally.

2 Add flour, half & half, clam juice, minced clams, and seafood or crab seasoning. Leave pot uncovered. **Select Auto-iQ Layered Bowls: Recipe 32 and press the START/STOP button.** Stir and serve.

SWAPS

Pancetta for bacon

Idaho potatoes for Yukon gold potatoes

CASHEW-CRUSTED FLOUNDER (DF)

PREP: 20 MINUTES | **COOK:** 27 MINUTES | **MAKES:** 4 SERVINGS

INGREDIENTS

1 tablespoon canola oil

3 cloves garlic, peeled, minced

1/2 bag (8 ounces) chopped kale

3 cups water, divided

4 uncooked flounder fillets (4 ounces each)

1 tablespoon kosher salt

2 tablespoons Dijon mustard

1/2 cup cashews, chopped

1 1/2 cups uncooked Israeli couscous

Juice of 1 lemon

OPTIONAL
1 tablespoon fresh chives, minced, for serving

DIRECTIONS

1 Set to STOVE TOP HIGH and preheat pot for 5 minutes. Heat oil in pot for 2 minutes and then add garlic, kale, and 1/2 cup water. Cook for 7 minutes, stirring occasionally. Season flounder with salt and brush with mustard, then gently cover with the chopped cashews.

2 Add remaining 2 1/2 cups water, couscous, and lemon juice to pot and stir to combine. Place crusted fish fillets on top, then cover pot. **Select Auto-iQ Layered Bowls: 33 and press the START/STOP button.** Stir and serve.

SWAP

Sole for flounder

RAVIOLI WITH MUSHROOM SAUCE (VG)

PREP: 10 MINUTES | **COOK:** 24 MINUTES | **MAKES:** 4–6 SERVINGS

INGREDIENTS

2 tablespoons olive oil

1/2 medium onion, peeled, diced

2 cloves garlic, peeled, crushed

2 1/2 cups vegetable stock

1 can (10 ounces) condensed cream of mushroom soup

1 package (8 ounces) sliced mushrooms

2 pounds frozen cheese ravioli

Tip: Garnish with 1/4 cup Romano cheese and 1 tablespoon fresh chopped parsley for a tasty topper and a pretty finished dish.

DIRECTIONS

1 Set to STOVE TOP HIGH and preheat pot for 5 minutes. Heat oil in pot for 2 minutes and then add onion and garlic. Sauté 2 minutes, or until onion is softened.

2 Add remaining ingredients to pot. Stir gently to combine, then cover pot. **Select Auto-iQ Layered Bowls: Recipe 34 and press the START/STOP button.** Serve immediately.

SWAP

Meat ravioli for cheese ravioli

MOROCCAN CHICKPEA STEW (GF) (DF) (VE)

PREP: 15 MINUTES | **COOK:** 47 MINUTES | **MAKES:** 6 SERVINGS

INGREDIENTS

1 1/2 tablespoons canola oil

2 medium carrots, peeled, chopped

1 medium onion, peeled, chopped

3 cloves garlic, peeled, minced

4 cups low-sodium vegetable broth

2 cans (15.5 ounces each) chickpeas, rinsed, drained

1 can (14.5 ounces) diced tomatoes

3 cups fresh baby spinach

1/2 cup uncooked long grain brown rice

1 teaspoon ground cumin

3/4 teaspoon ground ginger

1/4 teaspoon ground cinnamon

1/4 teaspoon crushed red pepper

DIRECTIONS

1 Set to STOVE TOP HIGH and preheat pot for 5 minutes. Heat oil in pot for 2 minutes and then add carrots, onion, and garlic. Cook uncovered for 5 minutes, stirring occasionally.

2 Add remaining ingredients to pot. Stir to combine, then cover pot. **Select Auto-iQ Layered Bowls: Recipe 35 and press the START/STOP button.** Serve immediately.

SWAPS

Cannellini beans for chickpeas

Kale for spinach

Meal need to be cooked a little longer? Simply set to BAKE DRY at 350°F for 5–10 minutes, checking for desired doneness.

KITCHEN BASICS 2.0

MANUAL RECIPES

There's a reason some cooking methods are classic—they work. We've taken these fundamental kitchen techniques and put them all in one convenient countertop device. Use the STOVE TOP, STEAM, BAKE, and SLOW COOK buttons on your Auto-iQ™ Cooking System to make everything from braised beef to steamed mussels, easy.

CHICKEN SATAY

PREP: 10 MINUTES | **COOK:** 23 MINUTES | **MAKES:** 8 SERVINGS

INGREDIENTS

16 wooden skewers

1 pound uncooked boneless, skinless chicken tenderloins, cut in half lengthwise

¼ teaspoon cayenne pepper

½ teaspoon ground ginger

Salt and black pepper, to taste

2 tablespoons canola oil

2 cloves garlic, peeled, minced

1 can (14 ounces) coconut milk

3 tablespoons creamy peanut butter

1 ½ tablespoons reduced-sodium soy sauce

3 tablespoons packed light brown sugar

OPTIONAL
Fresh cilantro leaves, for garnish

DIRECTIONS

1 Spray skewers with cooking spray. Thread chicken onto skewers. Season with cayenne pepper, ginger, salt, and black pepper.

2 Set to STOVE TOP HIGH and preheat pot for 5 minutes. Heat oil in pot for 2 minutes and then add garlic. Cook uncovered 1 minute or until garlic is tender, stirring often. Stir coconut milk, peanut butter, soy sauce, and brown sugar into pot. Season with salt and black pepper.

3 Place skewers on rack. Place rack in pot. Set to BAKE DRY at 325°F for 10 minutes, cover, and cook until chicken is cooked through. Remove skewers from pot, cover, and keep warm.

4 Reduce coconut milk mixture to a sauce by simmering on STOVE TOP LOW uncovered 5 minutes or until thickened, stirring often.

5 Sprinkle skewers with cilantro and serve with sauce.

HEARTY SKILLET LASAGNA

PREP: 5 MINUTES | **COOK:** 30-35 MINUTES | **MAKES:** 6 SERVINGS

INGREDIENTS

1 pound uncooked lean ground beef

10 uncooked lasagna noodles, broken in 2-inch pieces

1 jar (24 ounces) pasta sauce

1 1/2 cups water

1 package (about 6 ounces) fresh baby spinach

1 cup shredded mozzarella cheese

1/2 cup ricotta cheese

1/4 cup shredded Parmesan cheese

DIRECTIONS

1 Set to STOVE TOP HIGH and preheat pot for 5 minutes. Then add beef. Cook uncovered 10 minutes or until beef is browned, stirring often.

2 Arrange noodle pieces over beef. Pour sauce and water over noodles. Set to BAKE DRY at 350°F. Cover and cook 15–20 minutes or until noodles are tender. Turn off pot.

3 Stir in spinach. Combine cheeses in bowl; spoon cheese mixture over noodle mixture. Cover and let stand.

> **Tip:** Replace ground beef with ground turkey or chicken and add 1 tablespoon olive oil to pot before browning.

PRIME RIB AU JUS

PREP: 10 MINUTES | **COOK:** 1 HOUR 25 MINUTES | **MAKES:** 4 SERVINGS

INGREDIENTS

1 uncooked beef
standing rib roast
(about 5 pounds)

Salt and pepper, to taste

1 tablespoon fresh
rosemary, chopped

4 cups beef broth

1 tablespoon butter,
softened

1 tablespoon
all-purpose flour

DIRECTIONS

1 Season beef with salt, pepper, and rosemary.
Set pot to STOVE TOP HIGH and preheat pot
for 5 minutes. Add beef and cook uncovered
10 minutes or until browned on all sides.
Remove beef from pot.

2 Pour broth into pot. Place rack in pot. Place beef
on rack. Set to BAKE DRY at 350°F for 1 hour.
Cover and cook 1 hour for a medium-rare degree
of doneness. Transfer beef to a cutting board and
cover with foil.

3 Combine butter and flour in a bowl. Add mixture to
pot. Set to STOVE TOP HIGH. Cook 10 minutes or
until mixture is slightly reduced, stirring constantly.
Serve sauce with beef.

COD WITH ORANGE
GLAZE & SNAP PEAS

(DF) (A)

PREP: 5 MINUTES | **COOK:** 30 MINUTES | **MAKES:** 4 SERVINGS

INGREDIENTS

2 teaspoons canola oil

1 teaspoon
ground ginger

2 cloves garlic,
peeled, minced

1 bunch green onions,
sliced, divided

2/3 cup orange juice

1/3 cup water

2 teaspoons
low-sodium
soy sauce

1 tablespoon sugar

4 frozen uncooked
cod fillets, 1-inch thick

2 cups sugar snap peas

*Tip: Frozen cod comes in different weights and
thicknesses. For fish thicker than a 1/2 inch, add
an additional 1/2 cup water or orange juice to the
glaze, and add 2-4 minutes to the cooking time.*

DIRECTIONS

1 Set to STOVE TOP HIGH and preheat pot for
5 minutes. Heat oil in pot for 2 minutes. Add
ginger, garlic, and half the green onions to pot.
Cook uncovered 3 minutes or until garlic is tender,
stirring occasionally.

2 Stir orange juice, water, soy sauce, and sugar into
pot. Place frozen fish in a 9.75 x 7.25-inch pan.
Place rack in pot. Place pan on rack. Cover and
set to BAKE STEAM at 325°F for 15 minutes.

3 Place snap peas on top of fish. Cover and cook
5 minutes or until fish flakes easily when tested with
fork and snap peas are tender-crisp. Serve with
orange sauce and remaining green onions.

BANANA LIME COCONUT BREAD

PREP: 10 MINUTES | **COOK:** 40 MINUTES | **MAKES:** 10 SERVINGS

INGREDIENTS

1 cup all-purpose flour

1 1/2 teaspoons baking soda

1/4 teaspoon salt

1/2 ripe banana, mashed

2/3 cup skim milk

1 teaspoon vanilla extract

Zest and juice of 2 limes, divided

1/4 cup butter, divided

1/2 cup sugar

1 egg

4 cups water

1/3 cup toasted pecans, chopped

1/3 cup sweetened flaked coconut

1/4 cup packed brown sugar

DIRECTIONS

1 Spray a 6.5 x 11-inch loaf pan with cooking spray; set aside.

2 Combine flour, baking soda, and salt in a mixing bowl.

3 In another mixing bowl, combine banana, milk, vanilla extract, and half the lime zest and juice.

4 In another mixing bowl, beat 2 tablespoons butter and granulated sugar with an electric mixer until well combined. Beat in the egg.

5 Stir half the flour mixture and half the banana mixture into the butter mixture. Repeat with remaining flour mixture and butter mixture. Pour batter into loaf pan.

6 Pour water into pot. Place rack in pot. Place loaf pan on rack. Set to BAKE STEAM at 375°F for 40 minutes. Cover and cook until wooden toothpick inserted in center comes out clean. Remove pan from pot. Let bread cool in loaf pan on cooling rack for 10 minutes.

7 Use oven mitts to carefully remove rack from pot and pour out water. Combine remaining lime zest and juice, remaining butter, pecans, coconut, and brown sugar in pot. Set to STOVE TOP HIGH. Cook uncovered 1 minute or until sugar is dissolved. Spoon coconut mixture over bread.

CANTONESE STEAMED CHICKEN

(DF) A

PREP: 5 MINUTES | **COOK:** 33 MINUTES | **MAKES:** 4 SERVINGS

INGREDIENTS

2 tablespoons
soy sauce

1 tablespoon rice
wine vinegar

1 tablespoon fresh
ginger, minced

1 tablespoon honey

1/4 teaspoon crushed
red pepper

4 uncooked chicken
breasts, thinly sliced
(about 1 pound)

1 tablespoon
vegetable oil

1 medium onion,
peeled, sliced

2 carrots, peeled,
sliced 1/4-inch thick

1/2 cup chicken broth

1 pound sugar snap
peas, strings removed

6 shiitake mushrooms,
sliced, stems removed

DIRECTIONS

1 Stir soy sauce, vinegar, ginger, honey, and crushed
red pepper in a bowl. Add chicken and toss to coat.

2 Set to STOVE TOP HIGH and preheat pot for
5 minutes. Heat oil in pot for 2 minutes. Add onion
and carrots and cook uncovered 7 minutes, stirring
occasionally.

3 Remove chicken from soy sauce mixture and place
on rack.

4 Pour soy sauce mixture and chicken broth into
pot with onion and carrots. Cover and set to STEAM
for 5 minutes (steaming time) and wait for the beep
(approximately 7 minutes) to signify liquid
is boiling.

5 When beep sounds, use oven mitts to carefully
place rack in pot and cover. Steam 5 minutes.

6 Remove cover, add sugar snap peas and
mushrooms, and steam another 7 minutes until
chicken is cooked through and vegetables are
just tender.

7 At the second beep, use oven mitts to carefully
remove rack. Serve with the vegetables and
steaming liquid from the pot.

GARLIC LEMON STEAMED CLAMS

PREP: 5 MINUTES | **COOK:** 31 MINUTES | **MAKES:** 4 SERVINGS

INGREDIENTS

2 tablespoons olive oil

1 small onion, peeled, chopped

$\frac{1}{4}$ teaspoon salt

3 cloves garlic, peeled, minced

1 cup beer

1 lemon, sliced

2 tablespoons fresh parsley, chopped

2 dozen clams, uncooked, scrubbed

DIRECTIONS

1 Set to STOVE TOP HIGH and preheat pot for 5 minutes. Heat oil in pot for 2 minutes. Add onion and salt to pot. Cook uncovered 6 minutes or until onions are tender, stirring occasionally.

2 Add garlic to pot. Cook uncovered 1 minute, stirring often.

3 Add beer, lemon, and parsley to pot and cover. Set to STEAM for 10 minutes (steaming time). Wait for the beep (approximately 7 minutes) to signify liquid is boiling.

4 At the beep, add clams to the broth and cover.

5 At the second beep, serve immediately.

MUSSELS FRA DIAVOLO

PREP: 5 MINUTES | **COOK:** 14 MINUTES | **MAKES:** 4 SERVINGS

INGREDIENTS

2 cups Fra Diavolo sauce

1 cup water

1 pound mussels, uncooked, cleaned, debearded

3 long hot peppers, sliced into rings

DIRECTIONS

1 Place Fra Diavolo sauce and water in pot, cover, and set to STEAM for 7 minutes (steaming time) and wait for the beep (approximately 7 minutes) to signify liquid is boiling.

2 At the first beep, place mussels in sauce and cover.

3 At the second beep, split sauce and mussels between 4 bowls and top with hot peppers.

ASPARAGUS WITH LEMON AIOLI (DF) (VG)

PREP: 10 MINUTES | **COOK:** 17 MINUTES | **MAKES:** 4 SERVINGS

INGREDIENTS

1 cup water

1 lemon

$1/3$ cup light mayonnaise

1 small clove garlic, peeled, minced

$1/4$ teaspoon salt

Ground black pepper, to taste

1 pound asparagus, trimmed

DIRECTIONS

1 Pour water into pot, cover, and set to STEAM for 10 minutes (steaming time) and wait for the beep (approximately 7 minutes) to signify water is boiling.

2 Meanwhile, for the lemon aioli, grate $1/2$ teaspoon zest and squeeze 2 teaspoons juice from lemon into a bowl. Stir in mayonnaise, garlic, and salt. Season with black pepper.

3 Place asparagus on rack. At the first beep, use oven mitts to carefully place rack in pot and cover.

4 At the second beep, use oven mitts to carefully remove rack. Serve with lemon aioli.

CORN ON THE COB

(GF) (VG)

PREP: 5 MINUTES | **COOK:** 13 MINUTES | **MAKES:** 4 SERVINGS

INGREDIENTS

1 cup water

4 ears corn

1/4 cup garlic & herb cheese spread, divided

Salt and pepper, to taste

DIRECTIONS

1 Pour water into pot, cover, and set to STEAM for 6 minutes (steaming time) and wait for the beep (approximately 7 minutes) to signify water is boiling.

2 Meanwhile, pull back the husks of the corn (but do not remove), remove the silks, and then enclose corn with husks.

3 Place corn on rack. At the first beep, use oven mitts to carefully place rack in pot and cover.

4 At the second beep, use oven mitts to carefully remove rack.

5 Pull back husks and slather each ear with 1 tablespoon cheese spread, season with salt and pepper, replace husks, and serve immediately.

SAVORY POT ROAST

PREP: 20 MINUTES | **COOK:** 6-8 HOURS | **MAKES:** 8 SERVINGS

INGREDIENTS

1 uncooked boneless beef chuck roast (3 to 4 pounds)

$1/4$ cup plus 2 tablespoons flour, divided

$1/4$ cup olive oil, divided

2 carrots, peeled, chopped

2 stalks celery, chopped

1 medium onion, peeled, chopped

3 cloves garlic, peeled, crushed

1 can (28 ounces) whole plum tomatoes in purée

1 cup red wine

1 cup beef broth

3 sprigs fresh thyme

2 sprigs fresh rosemary

1 tablespoon butter, softened

DIRECTIONS

1 Coat beef with $1/4$ cup flour.

2 Set to STOVE TOP HIGH and preheat pot for 5 minutes. Heat oil in pot for 2 minutes. Add beef to pot. Cook uncovered 10 minutes or until browned on all sides. Remove beef from pot.

3 Add remaining oil, carrots, celery, onion, and garlic to pot. Cook uncovered 10 minutes or until vegetables are tender, stirring occasionally. Add tomatoes, wine, broth, thyme, and rosemary and heat to a boil.

4 Return beef to pot. Set to SLOW COOK LOW for 6–8 hours. Cover and cook until beef is fork-tender.

5 Transfer beef to cutting board. Combine butter and remaining flour in a bowl, then stir into pot. Set to STOVE TOP HIGH. Cook uncovered 2 minutes or until gravy is thickened.

6 Serve beef with gravy.

KOREAN CHICKEN WINGS

PREP: 10 MINUTES | **COOK:** 3-5 HOURS | **MAKES:** 4 SERVINGS

(DF)

INGREDIENTS

2 pounds uncooked chicken wings, tips removed

$1/2$ cup soy sauce

$1/4$ cup packed brown sugar

3 cloves garlic, peeled, minced

2 tablespoons fresh ginger, minced

3 green onions, thinly sliced

DIRECTIONS

1 Set to STOVE TOP HIGH and preheat pot for 5 minutes. Add chicken to pot. Cook uncovered 5 minutes or until chicken is lightly browned on both sides.

2 Stir soy sauce, brown sugar, garlic, ginger, and green onions in bowl. Pour mixture over chicken and toss to coat. Set to SLOW COOK LOW and cook covered for 3–5 hours.

Tip: Preparing for a crowd? Double the recipe and keep wings warm in the pot on SLOW COOK WARM for the duration of your party.

PULLED PORK & APPLE CIDER SLIDERS

(DF) (A)

PREP: 10 MINUTES | **COOK:** 5-6 HOURS | **MAKES:** 6 SERVINGS

INGREDIENTS

1 uncooked boneless pork shoulder roast (3 to 4 pounds)

Salt and pepper, to taste

2 teaspoons paprika

1/4 cup spicy brown mustard

1/4 cup packed brown sugar

3 cloves garlic, peeled, minced

1 cup apple cider or apple juice

12 slider or mini sandwich buns

DIRECTIONS

1 Season pork with salt, pepper, and paprika. Stir mustard, brown sugar, garlic, and cider in pot. Add pork and turn to coat. Set to SLOW COOK HIGH for 5–6 hours. Cover and cook until pork is fork-tender.

2 Transfer pork to a large bowl, and use two forks to shred it. Divide pork among buns.

HEARTY BEEF STEW

(DF)

PREP: 10 MINUTES | **COOK:** 7-9 HOURS | **MAKES:** 8 SERVINGS

INGREDIENTS

2 pounds uncooked
stew beef

1 teaspoon salt

1/2 teaspoon ground
black pepper

1/4 cup all-purpose flour

2 tablespoons
vegetable oil

1 1/2 cups beef broth

4 red potatoes,
cut in quarters

2 onions, peeled,
cut in quarters

1 cup baby carrots

4 cloves garlic,
peeled, chopped

2 sprigs fresh thyme
(or 1 teaspoon
dried thyme leaves,
crushed)

1 cup frozen peas,
thawed

DIRECTIONS

1 Season beef with salt and black pepper.
Coat with flour.

2 Set to STOVE TOP HIGH and preheat pot for
5 minutes. Heat oil in pot for 2 minutes. Add beef
and cook uncovered 10 minutes or until browned,
stirring occasionally.

3 Stir broth, potatoes, onions, carrots, garlic, and
thyme into pot. Set to SLOW COOK LOW for 7–9
hours. Cover and cook until beef is fork-tender.
Stir in peas during last 10 minutes of cooking time.

PORK CHOPS PROVENÇAL

(GF) (DF) (PA) (A)

PREP: 15 MINUTES | **COOK:** 5-7 HOURS | **MAKES:** 6 SERVINGS

INGREDIENTS

1/4 pound bacon,
cut in 1-inch strips

6 uncooked bone-in
center-cut pork chops

Salt and ground black
pepper, to taste

1 large onion,
peeled, thinly sliced

3 cloves garlic,
peeled, minced

1 can (14.5 ounces)
diced tomatoes

1 package (8 ounces)
frozen artichoke hearts,
thawed, drained

1 cup Kalamata olives,
pits removed

1 tablespoon fennel seed

DIRECTIONS

1 Set to STOVE TOP HIGH and preheat pot for
5 minutes. Add bacon. Cook uncovered 10 minutes
or until bacon is crisp, stirring occasionally. Remove
bacon from pot and drain on paper towels.

2 Season pork with salt and black pepper. Add
pork to pot. Cook 10 minutes or until browned
on both sides.

3 Return bacon to pot. Add onion, garlic, tomatoes,
artichoke hearts, olives, and fennel seed to pot.
Cook 5 minutes, stirring occasionally. Set to SLOW
COOK LOW for 5–7 hours. Cover and cook until
pork is fork-tender.

EGGS BENEDICT

PREP: 20 MINUTES | **COOK:** 35 MINUTES | **MAKES:** 3 SERVINGS

(GF)

INGREDIENTS

3 English muffins, cut in half

6 slices Canadian bacon

6 poached eggs (see PROGRAM 3, page 20)

1 cup Hollandaise sauce (see below)

OPTIONAL
1 tablespoon chives, minced, for garnish

HOLLANDAISE SAUCE

3 egg yolks

¼ cup lemon juice

1 teaspoon kosher salt

2 sticks (1 cup) butter, melted

DIRECTIONS

1 To make the Hollandaise Sauce, set to STOVE TOP HIGH and immediately add egg yolks, lemon juice, and salt. Whisk constantly for 1 minute, or until egg mixture is frothy. For 2 minutes, slowly whisk in the melted butter, ensuring it is evenly distributed and emulsified with the eggs. Use oven mitts to carefully remove the pot from the unit, then whisk in warm water to thin sauce, if needed. Transfer sauce to a bowl.

2 Place the English muffins and Canadian bacon on a baking sheet and toast in the oven for 5 minutes at 375°F.

3 To poach the eggs, use Auto-iQ Poached Infusions Program 3 (see page 20).

4 To assemble the Eggs Benedict, place one slice of Canadian bacon on each half of the toasted English muffins. Lay a poached egg on top of each piece of bacon, and then cover generously with Hollandaise Sauce. Garnish with minced chives and serve.

Tip: Use Hollandaise Sauce to top steak, potatoes, asparagus, or other vegetables.

Tip: Get creative with your Eggs Benedict by using lobster meat, crab meat, smoked salmon, or hash in place of the Canadian Bacon.

BUTTERNUT SQUASH RISOTTO WITH BACON & SAGE

A

PREP: 25 MINUTES | **COOK:** 62 MINUTES | **MAKES:** 6 SERVINGS

INGREDIENTS

1 tablespoon olive oil

2 medium onions, peeled, chopped

4 strips uncooked bacon, chopped

2 tablespoons fresh sage, chopped

1 cup uncooked Arborio rice

$1/2$ teaspoon salt

$1/4$ teaspoon ground black pepper

4 cups chicken broth

2 cups butternut squash, peeled, chopped

$1/4$ cup grated Parmesan cheese

DIRECTIONS

1 Set to STOVE TOP HIGH and preheat pot for 5 minutes. Heat oil in pot for 2 minutes. Add onions, bacon, and sage to pot. Cook uncovered 10 minutes or until onions are tender, stirring occasionally.

2 Stir rice, salt, and pepper into pot. Cook uncovered 5 minutes, stirring often.

3 Stir in broth. Cook 10 minutes.

4 Stir squash into pot. Set to STOVE TOP LOW. Cover and cook 20 minutes or until rice and squash are tender.

5 Stir cheese into pot. Set to STOVE TOP HIGH. Cook uncovered 10 minutes or until liquid is absorbed and mixture is creamy, stirring occasionally.

MINI CHEESECAKES

(VG)

PREP: 15 MINUTES | **COOK:** 35 MINUTES | **CHILL:** 3 HOURS | **MAKES:** 2 5-INCH SPRINGFORM PANS

INGREDIENTS

½ cup graham cracker crumbs

2 tablespoons butter, melted

⅓ cup sugar, divided

1 ½ packages (12 ounces) cream cheese, softened

1 egg

1 teaspoon vanilla extract

Zest of 2 lemons

4 cups water, room temperature

DIRECTIONS

1 Cover outside of 2 (5-inch) springform pans with foil. In a medium bowl, combine graham cracker crumbs, melted butter, and 1 tablespoon sugar. Press mixture into bottom of springform pans.

2 In a large bowl, beat cream cheese and remaining sugar with an electric mixer or handheld whisk until smooth. Beat in egg, vanilla extract, and lemon zest. Pour batter evenly into pans.

3 Pour water into pot. Place rack in pot and place pans on rack. Cover and set to STOVE TOP HIGH. Cook for 35 minutes.

4 Use oven mitts to carefully remove the rack. Transfer cheesecakes to refrigerator and chill at least 3 hours.

Tip: Serve with fresh fruit tossed in sugar, fruit preserves, chocolate sauce, or chopped toasted nuts.

HARD-BOILED EGGS

GF DF VG PA

PREP: 2 MINUTES | **COOK:** 30 MINUTES | **MAKES:** 2–12 EGGS

INGREDIENTS

2–12 eggs

8 cups water

DIRECTIONS

1 Place desired number of eggs in the pot along with 8 cups of water. Set to STOVE TOP HIGH, cover, and cook for 30 minutes.

2 When finished, remove with a slotted spoon and serve immediately if desired, or cool down in ice water and store in the refrigerator up to 3 days.

Tip: To keep shells from cracking, add 1 tablespoon vinegar to the water.

Tip: Eat these plain with sea salt, or mash into egg salad with mayo and paprika.

SOFT-BOILED EGGS

GF DF VG PA

PREP: 2 MINUTES | **COOK:** 20 MINUTES | **MAKES:** 2–12 EGGS

INGREDIENTS

2–12 eggs

8 cups water

DIRECTIONS

1 Place desired number of eggs in the pot along with 8 cups of water. Set to STOVE TOP HIGH, cover, and cook for 20 minutes.

2 When finished, remove with a slotted spoon and serve immediately if desired, or cool down in ice water and store in the refrigerator up to 3 days.

Tip: To keep shells from cracking, add 1 tablespoon vinegar to the water.

MORE HELPFUL HOW-TOS

REFERENCE CHARTS

Exactly how long should you steam parsnips? Is slow cooking pork tenderloin different than slow cooking pork shoulder, and how different is it? What is hoisin sauce and where can I get it? You'll find the answers to all these and more in the next few pages. Happy cooking!

TAKE TASTE BUDS OFF THE BEATEN PATH

From garam masala to sambal oelek, here's a list of some ingredients you may not already have in your pantry and where to find them at your local supermarket.

INGREDIENT	WHAT IT IS	WHERE TO FIND IT
Garam Masala	A blend of spices used in India, Pakistan, and other South Asian cuisine, typically composed of peppercorn, clove, cinnamon, mace, cardamom, bay leaf, and cumin	Herbs and spices section
Curry Paste	A staple of Thai cuisine, usually composed of shrimp paste, lemongrass, green Thai chili pepper, peppercorn, garlic, lime, cumin, coriander, and galangal	Sauces section
Hoisin Sauce	A sauce used in many Chinese dishes, usually made of black bean sauce, sugar, garlic, vinegar, and five-spice powder	Sauces section of the International food aisle
Lemongrass	A type of grass commonly used in Thai and Vietnamese cuisine, known for its mild citrusy flavor	Produce section
Mirin	A rice wine used in Japanese cooking, with a sweet flavor, slightly thick consistency, and golden to light amber color	Sauces section of the International food aisle
Okra	A vegetable that looks like a ridged pepper and when cooked, releases a gelatin-like substance that makes it a popular ingredient for gumbos and soups	Produce section
Sambal Oelek	A spicy Southeast Asian chile sauce made with hot red chile pepper, salt, vinegar, and sometimes onion, garlic, or sugar—spicier than Sriracha	Sauces section of the International food aisle

STEAM CHART

VEGETABLE	SIZE/PREPARATION	WATER	SEASONING IDEAS	STEAMING TIME
Artichokes	whole	4 cups	olive oil, lemon zest	25–40 minutes
Asparagus	whole spears	3 cups	olive oil	7–13 minutes
Beans, green	whole	2 cups	garlic, minced	6–10 minutes
Beans, wax	whole	2 cups	Italian seasoning	6–10 minutes
Beets	whole, unpeeled	4 cups	garlic, minced	35–50 minutes
Beet greens	coarsely chopped	2 cups	thyme	7–9 minutes
Broccoli	trimmed stalks	2 cups	olive oil	1–5 minutes
Broccoli	florets	2 cups	olive oil	5–7 minutes
Brussels sprouts	whole, trimmed	3 cups	thyme	8–15 minutes
Cabbage	cut in wedges	2 cups	lemon juice	6–10 minutes
Carrots	¼ inch slices	2 cups	maple syrup	7–10 minutes
Carrots, baby	whole	2 cups	honey and ginger	7–10 minutes
Cauliflower	florets	2 cups	lemon juice	5–10 minutes
Corn on the cob	whole, husks removed	2 cups	garlic butter	15–20 minutes
Kale	trimmed	2 cups	olive oil and garlic	5–8 minutes
Okra	whole, trimmed	2 cups	sautéed scallions	6–8 minutes
Onions, pearl	whole	2 cups	lemon juice	8–12 minutes
Parsnips	peeled, ½ inch slices	2 cups	Italian seasoning	7–10 minutes
Peas, green	fresh or frozen shelled	2 cups	mint and lemon juice	2–4 minutes
Peas, sugar snap	whole pods, trimmed	2 cups	mint and lemon juice	5–6 minutes
Potatoes, all	½ inch slices	2 cups	parsley dill	8–12 minutes
Potatoes, new	whole	4 cups	parsley or rosemary	15–20 minutes
Potatoes, sweet	½ inch chunks	3 cups	honey	8–12 minutes
Spinach	whole leaves	2 cups	olive oil and garlic	3–5 minutes
Squash, butternut	peeled, ½ inch cubes	2 cups	maple syrup	7–10 minutes
Turnips	½ inch slices	3 cups	Italian seasoning	8–12 minutes
Turnip greens	coarsely chopped	2 cups	olive oil and garlic	4–8 minutes
Swiss Chard	coarsely chopped	2 cups	olive oil and garlic	3–5 minutes
Zucchini	1 inch slices	2 cups	olive oil and Italian seasoning	5–8 minutes

SLOW COOK CHART

TYPE OF MEAT	COOK TIME LOW	COOK TIME HIGH
BEEF		
Top or bottom round	8–10 hours	4–5 hours
Eye of the round	6–8 hours	3–4 hours
Chuck	8–10 hours	4–5 hours
Pot roast or brisket	7–9 hours	$3\frac{1}{2}$–$4\frac{1}{2}$ hours
Short ribs	7–9 hours	$3\frac{1}{2}$–$4\frac{1}{2}$ hours
Frozen meatballs (precooked)	6–8 hours	3–4 hours
PORK		
Baby back or country ribs	7–9 hours	$3\frac{1}{2}$–$4\frac{1}{2}$ hours
Pork tenderloin	6–7 hours	3–4 hours
Pork loin or rib roast	7–9 hours	$3\frac{1}{2}$–$4\frac{1}{2}$ hours
Pork butt or shoulder	10–12 hours	5–6 hours
Ham, bone in (uncooked)	7–9 hours	$3\frac{1}{2}$–$4\frac{1}{2}$ hours
Ham (fully cooked)	5–7 hours	$2\frac{1}{2}$–$3\frac{1}{2}$ hours
POULTRY		
Boneless, skinless breast	6–7 hours	3–4 hours
Boneless, skinless thighs	6–$7\frac{1}{2}$ hours	3–$4\frac{1}{2}$ hours
Bone-in breast	6–$7\frac{1}{2}$ hours	3–$4\frac{1}{2}$ hours
Bone-in thighs	7–9 hours	$3\frac{1}{2}$–$4\frac{1}{2}$ hours
Whole chicken	7–9 hours	$3\frac{1}{2}$–$4\frac{1}{2}$ hours
Chicken wings	6–7 hours	3–4 hours
Turkey breast or thighs	7–9 hours	$3\frac{1}{2}$–$4\frac{1}{2}$ hours
FISH		
1-inch fillets	N/A	30–45 minutes
OTHER		
Stew meat (beef, lamb, veal, rabbit)	7–9 hours	3–4 hours

INDEX

INDEX